BOHEMIA
INTERNATIONAL

History
of Czechoslovakia
in Outline

T. G. Masaryk
A statue by Jan Štursa, bronze

J. V. Polišenský

HISTORY OF CZECHOSLOVAKIA IN OUTLINE

BOHEMIA INTERNATIONAL

ISBN 80-85195-05-04

PREFACE

Between 1938 and 1945 many books and pamphlets about Czechoslovakia were published in England, most of them propaganda either for or against the Czechoslovak State. Today the Czechoslovak State has been restored to its ancient frontiers and liberties and has for two years pursued quietly and in good order the task of recovery and reconstitution. It has fallen somewhat out of the concern of the British press and the British people, largely just because of the success of President Beneš and the Czechoslovak government in their aim to make the country an oasis of order and efficient democracy in Central Europe.

But we in Britain should not forget Czechoslovakia, for the role it has to play in the future is important, and it is the role that the Czechoslovak people has so often played in the past: that of providing a bridge between the civilizations of East and West, in both of which it shares.

For this reason I welcome this little book by Dr Polišenský. When I heard, in London in the autumn of 1946, the three lectures on which it was based, I was convinced that the clarity, succintness and impartiality with which he dealt with the theme made it desirable that it should be published, to keep the British people not to forget the contribution to European civilization which the Czechoslovak people has made, as an earnest of what they may be able to contribute in the years ahead.

Prague-April 1947

R. R. BETTS

Masaryk Professor of Central European History-
School of Slavonic and East European Studies-
London University

After six years of oppression Czechoslovakia enters a new period of her history. Her people and their government are trying to realise what preceding generations longed for: to secure political liberty and social justice. It is not seldom that an observer, especially if he stands outside the territory of Czechoslovakia, finds it puzzling that either of these should need accentuating in defining a state's aims. This outline of the history of Czechoslovakia endeavours to show him the historical background of the network of problems of today, and to win his understanding, if not his friendly feeling.

Yet can Czechoslovak history be treated as a whole, when the existence of two national units, the Czechs and the Slovaks, has been expressly recognised? Observers from abroad, especially if they are members of big nations, are apt to exaggerate the importance of the separation of the Czechs and Slovaks. Since the days of the Romantic movement there have been tendencies in the history of Europe to create big national and political wholes, as there have been tendencies to disintegrate such wholes and thus give independent existence to minor national units. For a full hundred years the Czechs and Slovaks have lived side by side, bound by the close tie of a kindred language and a thousand years of common culture. There is not and has never been a clear boundary line, in language and ethnology, between the two. The fact that it was not until united in one republican state that Bohemia and Moravia on the one hand and Slovakia on the other had all boundaries between them blotted out appears less important when we realise that in the course of the past eleven centuries these lands had a common ruler for as long as six hundred years. Beside the common literary tradition the influence of a uniform development of culture has always been at work. One cannot find any clear-cut dividing lines in the culture of the two peoples. There is rather a sort of inter-

penetration of ethnical elements, and what a fortunate give and take it is, considering that to it Czechoslovakia owes her creator T. G. Masaryk, a native of Moravia and descendant of Slovak serfs! The cultural correspondence is naturally based on a correspondence of social development, a circumstance evidenced by the fact that in the last three centuries the nation and her aspirations in Bohemia and Moravia as well as in Slovakia have been represented by the common people. The Czechoslovak people, a unit, ethnical, cultural, and today political as well, is to be, properly speaking, the hero of the present history.

I

THE ORIGINS OF LAND AND PEOPLE

The country is older than its present inhabitants. Bohemia, Moravia and Slovakia are, from the standpoint of political geography, one entire territory, situated along the watershed of the rivers that feed the European seas. The Labe and the Odra rise there, but so do the Morava and the Váh. The border mountains have never been a serious obstacle to the development of communications running from east to west, and the lowlands on both sides of the big rivers were a good continuation of the tracks and roads heading from the Adriatic across the Alps to the North. No wonder that this natural centre intersected by all cultural trends has from old times been part of the territory used for human settlement. In the days when the human race in Europe showed progress in development only along the Rhine and in the British Isles, Moravia began to emerge from the darkness of the prehistoric past. No splendid cave drawings like those of Altamira were left there by the Palaeolithic Men, yet the artistic feeling of the race of old Moravia is unmistakably proved by the richness of plastic design in all the finds that have been made there to date. The valleys of the Moravian rivers were later inhabited by hunting tribes of Neolithic Men, whose artistic taste is, however, confined to ornaments on everyday crockery. Originating in Moravia, colonization came to Bohemia. Here the men coming from the east brought their knowledge of utilizing metals and after 2000 B. C. gave rise to one of the focal points of the culture of the Bronze Age, generally referred to by the name of the village of Únětice in Central Bohemia. In the 16th century B. C. there lived two different races in the territory of Bohemia. The one cremated, their dead, while the other buried them in mounds. The look of that country in those days was still far from the uniform whole shown by the map today.

Nor did it become a uniform whole later, when in the 5th century B. C. Celtic tribes settled down there after flooding the continent of Europe from the Balkans as far as the British Isles. The Celtic tribes of the Boii and the Cottini in Bohemia and Slovakia respectively left behind them a number of place-names, above all the name of Bohemia referring to the part of the territory bearing the vernacular name Čechy, and the names of the rivers Labe, corresponding to Celtic Albis (Albion) and mutated to Elbe in German, and Jizera, corresponding to the French Ysère. They also gave to the territory a town-dwelling culture, based on trade and industries. Thus the important finding-places of Stradonice in Bohemia and Hradisko in Moravia are not situated on old ways in riverside lowlands, but in woody regions in the neighbourhood of ore deposits. When the Central European domination of the Celts had been shaken by the Thracians, Germanic tribes began to penetrate into the territory from the west. The Germanic Marcomans in Bohemia and Quades in Slovakia were not numerous, or at least we know for sure that they occupied but a part of the territory, leaving old Celtic dwelling centres to fall to ruins. At about the time of Christ's birth, Marcoman tribes encountered the vanguards of the Roman Empire which, spreading northwards, had by that time reached the Danube. Some of the scenes represented on Trajanus' Column in Rome refer to the fights with the Marcomans. The Emperor Marcus Aurelius wrote his Meditations on the banks of the Hron in Slovakia, in those days about the centre of the Quade territory.

Neither Marcomans nor Romans left many traces of their settlement. There is a rock below Trenčín Castle in Slovakia with an inscription hewn by the soldiers of the Roman legions. They too built castella in the south of Moravia and Slovakia, representing single links in the chain of the "limes Romanus" running along the Danube.

The Romans did not succeed in crossing the borders of the basins of the Danube, Morava and Dyje. Thus a border line gradually came into existence that was to be the boundary of Czechoslovak territory facing south for a period of two thousand years. This fact is the more remarkable in that Bohemia was then no geographical whole, if we may judge from the first chart of these parts by Claudius Ptolemy in the 2nd century A. D., on which we miss the characteristic quadrangle of Bohemia but find the treble chain of the Hercynian Forest.

THE historie of BOHEMIA.

THE FIRST PARTE.

describing

THE COVNTRYE SCITVATI=
on, climate, commodities;
the name and nature of the people
AND COMPENDIOVSLY CONTINVĪG
the Historie from the begining of
the Nation to their first
Christian Prince a=
bout the yeare of
Christ
990

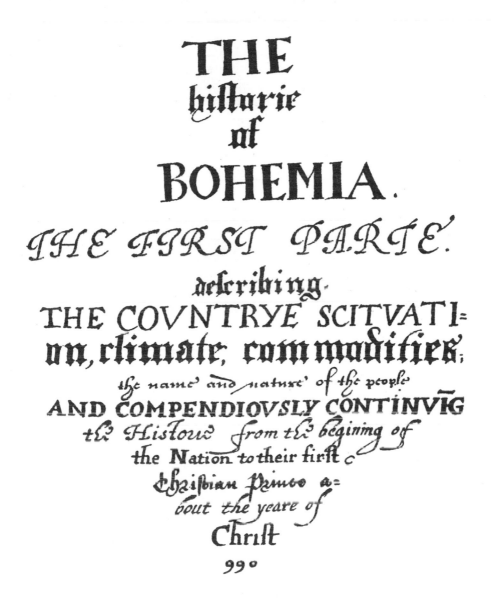

The Historie of Bohemia, A. D. 1619—20
From the Harleian MSS, the British Museum

When the invasion of the Goths into the territory of the Roman Empire indirectly caused the revolutionary Migration of Peoples, a new race entered the territory between the Sudeten Mountains, the Carpathians and the Danube, a territory not yet uniform in appearance but showing in outline the border lines later to come. They were the Slavs, and to all appearances they did not have to fight for the territory, as the Marcomans had long been gone at the time and their Germanic successors do not seem to have been numerous. The supposition that some Germanic tribes might have stayed in the territory of Bohemia without interruption, as the German propagandists would have it, lacks all foundation. There is not the slightest evidence to corroborate it.

Slavonic tribes, coming from the North East, gradually settled down in Bohemia, Moravia and, eventually, in Slovakia. Their original home was the one, common to all Indo-European peoples, in Central Asia, where they had been living a nomadic life. The old road of the Asiatic invader of Europe brought them to what nowadays is Southern Russia. On the extensive territory between the Volga and the Dnieper they met the more progressive Scyths and changed from nomadic to agricultural tribes. Pressed by the Scyths they proceeded further west into the woody tracts between the Dnieper, the Vistula and the Carpathians, the traditional home of all the Slavs. There they were found by the geographer, Claudius Ptolemy, who mentions the "immense nation" of Wends with undisguised respect.

There has never been a satisfactory solution offered to the problem of why and under what circumstances the parting of the Slavs took place. Our curiosity is too great to be satisfied with what research has so far discovered. Only the romantic idea of peace-loving Slavonic land-toilers oppressed by warlike nomads has been refuted, and thereby the theory that it was the nomadic Avars that brought the oppressed Slavs to their seats. Besides, both tribes entered Central European territory from different directions: the Slavs, from the north-east, the Avars, from the south-east. It remains a fact that in the last stormy period of the Migration of Peoples the Slavs moved first westwards and then southwards and eastwards. There are several other puzzling problems yet to be solved by historians, such as the explanation of the relation of Lusatian Serbia to the present Serbia, and that of the present Croatia to the tribes of Croats in what is now Eastern Bohemia and to White Croatia in Galicia.

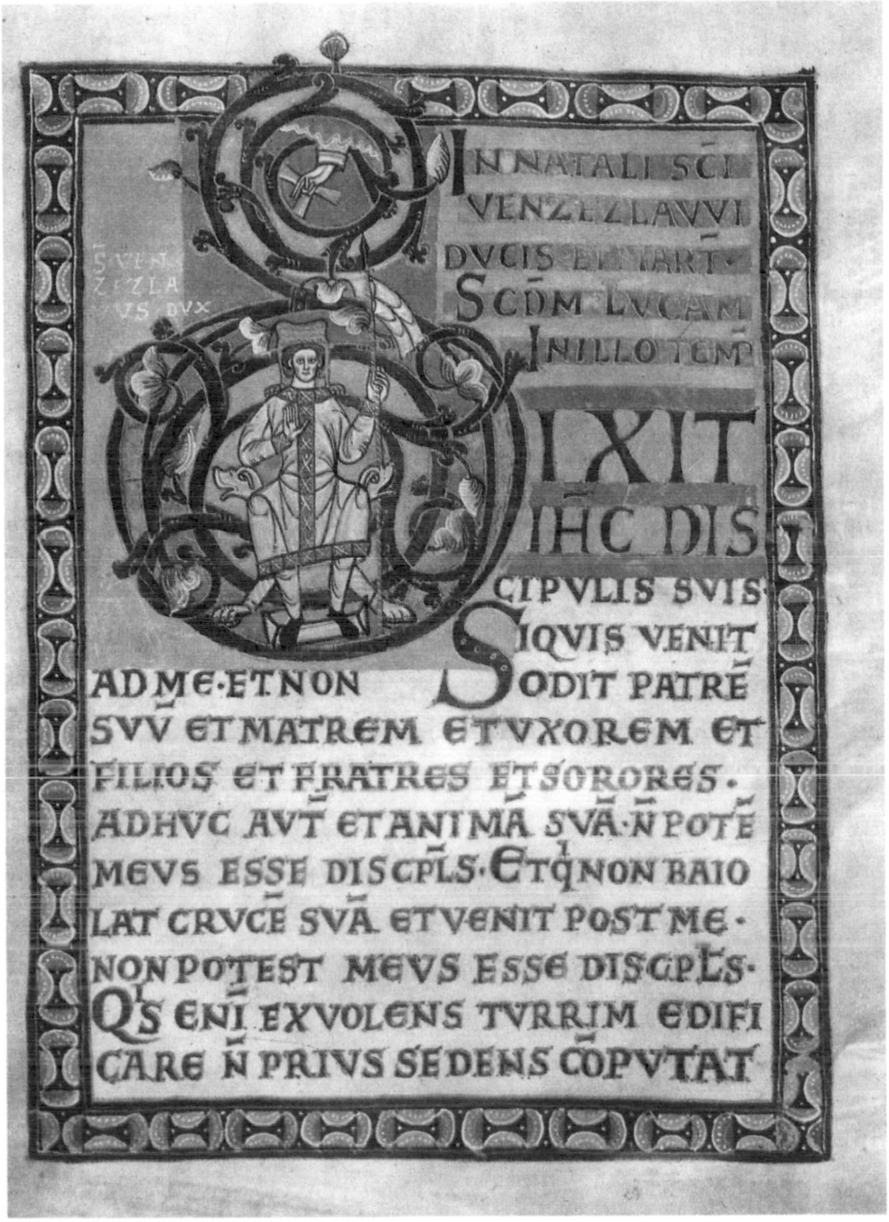
S VEN
ZEZLA
VS DVX
IN NATALI SCI
VENZEZLAVVI
DVCIS ET MART.
SCDM LVCAM
IN ILLO TEMP
DIXIT
IHC DIS
CIPVLIS SVIS.
SIQVIS VENIT
AD ME. ET NON ODIT PATRE
SVV ET MATREM ET VXOREM ET
FILIOS ET FRATRES ET SORORES.
ADHVC AVT ET ANIMA SVA. N POTE
MEVS ESSE DISCPLS. ET Q NON BAIO
LAT CRVCE SVA ET VENIT POST ME.
NON POTEST MEVS ESSE DISCPLS.
QS ENI EX VOLENS TVRRIM EDIFI
CARE N PRIVS SEDENS COPVTAT

Good King Wenceslas, the Patron Saint of Bohemia

The Codex of Vyšehrad, Initial D, A. D. 1086

In their new home the Slavs became dependent on the Avars, a circumstance attested by reliable sources. As early as 630 we find mention there of a rising of the Central European Slavs against the cruel oppressors who exercised rule all over their territory from what today is the Hungarian Lowland. Their rising, connected with the semi-mythical figure of the ruler Samo, met with success and the Central European Slavs turned against their western neighbours, the Franks, whose claims to sovereign rule were thus for the first time refuted. The fight to retain an independent existence has from the remotest past been one of the first tasks of the Slavs in Czechoslovak lands. This is corroborated by reports of the struggles between the re-created Roman Empire of Charlemagne and the Slavs of Bohemia. The mighty ruler, whose name (Carlo) served the Western Slavs for the term "king" (král, król), no doubt became the overlord of some, if not all, of the Slavonic tribes in Bohemia. Yet their territory never became an immediate dependency, nor did this supra-national romanized empire ever attempt to germanize the Bohemian Slavs, as the mercenary German historiographers have so often sweated to prove. The custom of paying a definite amount a year to the western neighbour apparently originated in this time. It was made infrequently and by way of token. There is no justification for ascribing its origin to Prince Wenceslas the Saint, as later tradition did.

Charlemagne had for good and all removed the threat of the Avars by ruining their domains in the Danubian basin. In this way the reunion of the western and the southern Slavs, as well as a tentative Slavonic state on the eastern border of Charlemagne's empire, was made possible. These attempts at unification sprang particularly from Moravia, that is, the basin of the Morava, where single tribes began to unite which until then had been independent and autonomous and only at a pinch, under the leadership of a provisional chief, had jointly defended the strongholds inhabited by themselves and their kin. Towards the end of the third decade of the 9th century the process of unification began to extend to the territory of the present Slovakia, where a native leader-prince of Nitra attempted by consenting to conversion to Christianity to obtain the help of the rulers of East Franconia. About fifteen years later, the leaders of the Bohemian tribes tried the same methods with equally poor success. The founder of the Great Moravian Empire, Mojmír I, gained influence in both the territories, and, deprived of his rule, through the jealousy of the heirs to Charlemagne, he left Rostislav, his nephew and successor, in carrying out the same plans. In Rostislav's reign the Great Moravian Empire came to the fore in the Europe of that time by alliance with Byzantium, then the most progressive part of the world. Thus the Great Moravian Empire and Byzantium stood in one line of defence against the Frankish Empire allied with the Bulgarians. In accordance with his general policy, Rostislav sent messengers to Byzantium in 863 to request the sending out of a Christian mission. The arrival of the Byzantine missionaries, Constantinus and Methodius, marks a turning point in the cultural development of the territory. With the introduction of a literary Slavonic language and one raised to the language of liturgy, the Czechoslovak lands joined on principles of parity the great community of Christian culture.

There is no doubt that this happened contrary to what the Germanic neighbour would have liked to see. Complaints of German clergy about Methodius' activities as well as an open struggle for suzerainty brought about the enthronement of a new ruler, Svatopluk. Yet not even he was willing to give in to the dictate of the jealous East Frankish neighbours. During his reign Methodius was made Archbishop of Pannonia and Svatopluk's state for some time came to enjoy the immediate protection of the Holy See. It extended into Bohemia, whose prince at that time accepted baptism, into the Basin of the Vistula and into Pannonia, an important territory in present-day Western Hungary, linking bridgewise the Western Slavs with the Slavonic tribesmen in the Balkans and with Byzantium. This link was maintained till Svatopluk's death and so was the whole of the Great Moravian Empire. Not until the reign of Svatopluk's successor, Mojmír II, did the first historical Slav state in Czechoslovak territory succumb to the concentrated attack of the Eastern Franks and the Magyar tribes that had settled down in the Danubian Basin and taken over the heritage of the Avars. Soon after the collapse of the Great Moravian Empire, the Empire of the Eastern Franks succumbed to the Magyar raiders.

II

THE RISE OF THE CZECH STATE

The importance of the Great Moravian Empire has often been overlooked by observers from abroad. They have missed the fact that Great Moravia was a political whole, in existence for eighty years, which gave a powerful impetus to the process of unification among the Slavonic tribes. A hereditary ruler supported the rise of a suite of warriors who were entrusted with military as well as administrative and judicial functions. All over the country strongpoints sprang up intended for permanent residence. With the arrival of Christianity they became the focal points of cultural and social progress.

The same observers have often missed the fact that the inheritance of Great Moravia was never destroyed for good and all. The region of the Bohemian princes was the political heir to Great Moravia and took over too the cultural inheritance of Old Slavonic literature. Legends, created in the territory of Bohemia or in any other Slavonic territory by people who had come from Bohemia, survived the tenth century and joined hands with the literature written in Latin. The court of the first Przemyslids, especially that of Wenceslas the Saint, bears witness to the vitality of this cultural symbiosis. It was only by the Great Schism of 1054 that Europe was divided into two antagonistic parts, and in Bohemia, which from the ecclesiastical and cultural point of view was a part of Western Europe, the tendency arose to cut all ties with the Byzantine and Slavonic schismatism.

The real political heir to Great Moravia appeared in the clan of Přemyslids, who originally dominated the Czech tribe that had obtained its name from the region between the Lower Vltava, the Elbe, the Ohře and the Berounka, called "dry lands" (Czachy). From this

The Přemyslid Cycle
From a wall painting, St. Catherine's Rotunda, Znojmo, A. D. 1134

central point the Přemyslid Princes residing in Prague made their importance felt in their relations to the minor tribes and gradually united the country. The process of unification was not unopposed. An episode from the life of Prince Wenceslas the Saint (the Good King Wenceslas of the English Christmas carol) shows the strife the Prince had to wage against centrifugal forces. Besides, there were minor quarrels between the sovereign and his suite of warriors who found a rival to Wenceslas in his brother Boleslav and succeeded in murdering Wenceslas on the 28th September, 929. That was the real reason of the crime, not perhaps the rivalry between the Christians and heathens, as the legends will have it, and still less the Prince's alleged Germanophile attitude, as some German historians of recent times have attempted to prove. Wenceslas is not and never has been a symbol of positive relations between the Czech and the Germans. On the contrary, from oldest times, popular tradition has portrayed him as defender of the Czech nation against the German onslaught. His greatness is to be seen in the ambition of his cultural achievements, to which the Prague Cathedral and the richness of the legends on himself bear witness. The striking greatness of the young sovereign's figure did not remain without effect after his death. It was this greatness that first helped to unite the whole country under the Saint's banner and thus became to the rest of Christendom the symbol of Christian Bohemia against which it was not possible to wage a crusade. Later on, Wenceslas became the patron saint of Bohemia to whom the Czechs of the 12th century, as well as the Hussites, and the Catholics of the Baroque period appealed for help.

The political ambition of the Czechs is later represented by Wenceslas' successor, Boleslav. His scheme of creating a Slavonic "Sclavinia" was thwarted by King Otto I, who at the time was laying the foundations of a new German Empire and could hardly bear a rival so near at hand. But the common fight of Boleslav and Otto I against the Hungarians, victorious in 955, brought about the liberation of Moravia as far as the Váh river and the extension of the Czech domain as far as Cracow. That at least was the situation described by Ibrahim Ibn Jacob, a Jewish trader, who in the middle of the tenth century visited Central Europe. He saw "the white Castle of Prague" and the magnificence of its market-place. All over the country he entered towns clustering around castles where slaves were bartered against furs, the most important item of the exports of those days. The thriving merchant warriors came to represent an independent class making the best of commerce as well as of agriculture. The collective character of agriculture of that time began to be replaced by individual farming. As the number of dependents on the warriors' estates gradually rose, the clan as a social unit began to disintegrate, for there was a substantial increase in the people of a standing lower than was that of the other free people, of course lower than the warriors', Czechs of the leading class, but higher than that of slaves.

The latest plan of Boleslav I, to make Prague the centre of a bishopric, was only realised by his son Boleslaus II in 973. The boundaries of the "Holy Prague" as we find them in an old document extended as far east as the Rivers Stryj and Bug. It was in this direction that the Przemyslid Bohemia tried to re-establish the connection with the Slavonic tribes who had been separated from them ever since the Hungarians had come in the way of their contact with Byzantium. The pious monks of Prague had long ago, on their way to Kiev, wandered through the extensive region of the Carpathians and there was a similar traffic in the opposite direction between Kiev and the Slavonic monastery established on the Sázava river in Central Bohemia. Now, in the reign of Boleslav II, this region came to be the scene of the encounter of the political ambitions of the Slavs of Bohemia and those of Poland. Dubravka, Boleslav I's daughter, was married to Mieszko I, Prince of Poland, and exerted herself admirably to spread Christian ideals in her new country. Her son, Boleslav the Bold, had plans suggesting those of his renowned grandfather.

At that time, about the year 1000, when pious Christians were waiting for the end of the thousand years of falsehood and the advent of Christ upon earth, the Přemyslid princes were trying to realize plans of more realism than piety. They thought about uniting the present-day Bohemia into one whole. Among the tribal princes only one was left who could still be considered a dangerous rival. He was the leader of the tribe of Slavník, who at that time dominated a great part of South and East Bohemia. This tribe gave Bohemia the second Bishop of Prague, St. Adalbert. The Přemyslid plan of uniting all Bohemia under their rule was realized in the end through barbarous methods of extirpation, in keeping with the spirit of the day. But what had been gained at home, had to be paid for by severe losses abroad.

St. Adalbert, the adherent of a reform of monastic life starting from the monastery of Cluny in Burgundy, had more than one clash with his semiheathen fellow-countrymen. Then, finding all his next of kin murdered, he left for abroad to stay there for the rest of his life as a missionary. He propagated Christianity in Poland and Hungary, and to his influence the rulers of both these countries owed their promotion to independent kings, a rank which was only attained by the ruler of Bohemia a hundred year s later. When the learned bishop Adalbert was killed in East Prussia, a cathedral was erected above his grave in the Polish town of Gniezno and the Polish ruler, Boleslav the Bold, for some time ruled from the Castle of Prague.

Boleslav's great plan of uniting the two regions, Poland and Bohemia, in one political whole, probably with Prague as administrative centre, was not realised in the end. The German King, Henry II, thwarted the union of the two countries by supporting the Przemyslid princes who had been expelled and enabling them to return to their country. Thus the opportunity of creating a great Slavonic whole to dominate all Central Europe was wasted, and, still worse, the Czech princes became bound to the German kings more than ever before and Moravia remained in Polish hands.

Only about 1030 was Moravia regained by the young Czech prince, Břetislav. Yet, it was not the former Moravia in her entirety, but only the territory marked off in the east by the ranges of the White and Little Carpathians and the Bezkyds. The Czech princes did not penetrate east of this line. The ancestors of the Slovaks of today thus became inhabitants of the Hungarian State, at the time on the way to being properly established by St. Stephen and though the difference in ethnical structure granted the North of Hungary, i. e. present-day Slovakia, a special status, which endured for centuries to come, the separation though lamentable was a reality.

Half a century after the attempts of Boleslav the Bold, Břetislav pointed the spearhead of his attack against Poland. It was his ambition, too, to combine both the territories, but although he reached Gniezno and transferred home the relics of St. Adalbert, his efforts towards uniting the two countries were thwarted by another German ruler, Henry III. Břetislav was successful in defeating the Germans near Brůdek in the Bohemian Forest in 1040, he exacted a promise from the Polish princes to agree to yearly payment of 500 marks of silver and 30 marks of gold in acknowledgement of the sovereignty of the Czech ruler over Silesia. But he was unable to create a large Slavonic state. He gave the Přemyslid domains a more solid shape, making them a state not very extensive, but important in position and influence.

This is not to say that Břetislav's successors had no ambitions. Their chief ambition was to attain the rank of king. Břetislav's son, Vratislav, attained this very soon, in 1085. Annalists praise him as fair and faithful to his promises, qualities rarely mentioned in those days. He endeavoured to strengthen the position of the Czech state. Family quarrels were the greatest obstacle to his endeavours. To break the resistance of the Bishop of Prague, his own brother, he founded a bishopric at Olomouc in Moravia and a chapter at Vyšehrad, the acropolis of Prague. But according to the laws of the country he could not prevent the dismemberment of the allotments to his relatives, or the quarrels that weakened the position of the whole country, since the German rulers were diligent to interfere in them whenever they could. The Czech warriors did not leave German interference unanswered, for they had only been waiting for the advent of Gothic ideals to assume the rank of noblemen. At the end of the 11th century unknown pilgrims transferred the relics of the Kiev saints Boris and Gleb to the Sázava monastery. Other monks brought later, at the end of the 12th century the news of the life and death of St. Thomas of Canterbury from the west. A national feeling gradually arose in the country, though it is in Latin works that it is first perceptible. The presence of the national feeling is unmistakable in the Chronicle of the first Czech historian, Canon Cosmas, written at the beginning of the 12th century. In those days, the language of the country makes its first shy appearance. It is no longer the Old Church Slavonic, but Old Czech, which in the song Hospodine, pomiluj ny (O Lord, be merciful) first dominated the churches. The reports of the great victory of Prince Soběslav I over the German Emperor Lothar at Chlumec in 1126 breathe a clearly national feeling.

It was not only the quarrels among the members of the ruling family that shook the existence of the Bohemian state, there were also strifes between the ruler and his warriors. Vladislav I, second of the Czech kings, crowned at Ratisbon in 1158 with the crown provided by the King of England Henry II, was strong enough to put forth again the claim of Bohemia for Silesia and to mix with the quarrels in Hungary. In order to keep his might within bounds, the German Emperor Friedrich Barbarossa, "the most German of the German Emperors of the Middle Ages", exerted his efforts to the utmost. To him it is due that the last thirty years of the 12th century are to be recorded as the most baleful and grim in Czech history. In order to ensure for himself an absolute freedom of influence in the territory of Bohemia, Barbarossa established what he believed to be permanent rivals to the Bohemian rulers in the bishops of Prague and the margraves of Moravia. As early as 1193 King Vladislav's son was dethroned because by his adventurous union with the English King Richard I Coeur de Lion he had threatened the Emperor. Four years later, the rebel prince again ascended the throne and as King Přemysl I led his kingdom out of slavery and humiliation.

III

THE PŘEMYSLID KINGDOM

King Přemysl's successful work is an appropriate example of how an outstanding individual can contribute to the progress of his country. His reign dates back to the period when a great social change was making itself felt. This change was caused by the development from an economy of barter to one of finance. His was a period when the struggle between the spiritual and the temporal powers flared up once more. Přemysl's predecessors had already joined in this struglge but on the whole they were too much bound up with the interests of the imperial party. The refractory Přemyslid did not engage himself on either side. His policy was independent. Without doubt it was successful. In 1204 the Pope declared the canonization of another Czech saint, St. Procopius. He was formerly Abbot of the Slavonic cloister of Sázava, and a legend relates of him that he had driven out German monks from it by force. In 1212 the young Emperor Frederic II granted Přemysl a great charter. At that time Frederic did not yet possess the Imperial Seal and confirmed the charter with the sign of the Sicilian Kingdom. Hence it is called the Golden Sicilian Bull, and became the basis of the future relationship between the Přemyslid State and the Roman Empire of the German nation. In it the Emperor acknowledged the hereditary dignity of the Bohemian Kings and the fact that only a king elected or accepted by the Bohemians could be recognised as sovereign and Elector by the Emperor. The age-long efforts of the German Emperors to subjugate the Czech countries were completely frustrated by this stroke. The struggle between temporal and spiritual powers, advantageous as it was to the Czech State abroad, led to a long quarrel between the King and the Primate of Prague.

Přemysl was supported by the Bishop of Olomouc, Robert the Englishman, and although he did not win, he was able to prevent the Crown from being weakened. But there was some disadvantage in it. A hierarchy as it was known in other European countries at the height of the Middle Ages did not arise in Bohemia. Only exceptionally did Czech spiritual dignitaries become Maecenases of the culture in their country. The country was badly in need of such cultural support, for the court was just then losing touch with the spirit of the people.

The court of Přemysl's son, Wenceslas I, was dominated by the fashions of chivalry and of the prevailing Gothic, which came to Bohemia by way of Germany. The influence of Italy can be found in the milieu of Wenceslas' sister, Princess Agnes. Agnes became bride of the Emperor's son, Henry, then of the English king, Henry III, but in the end she came to practise the ideals of St. Francis of Assisi. Thanks to her efforts, Prague acquired in her convent the first building in the Gothic style. The Czech crusading Order of the Cross and the Red Star was also founded by her. According to the ideals of Agnes, who was in correspondence with St. Clare, the purpose of the order was not to fight but to care for the welfare of the poor and destitute.

To Wenceslas' reign belongs the full swing of internal colonisation. The prevailing peace in the country and the changing economic situation led to efforts to raise the regular income of landlords by renting property on the land. The landlords, at first the convents and the spiritual dignitaries, later on the king and his nobles, tried to increase the acreage of cultivation. New villages in the border region and the interior began to spring up. Naturally it was necessary to give the new settlers some economic advantages which differentiated them from the inhabitants of the old villages. It was said that the new settlers had the "purchase or German right" in contrast with the old Slavonic right. The term "German right" was a technical term and villages which took their origin in a similar way in Germany got the so-called "Dutch right." The new settlers differed from the other inhabitants in a higher degree of local autonomy, in a more secure hold on the land and, finally, for them tithes were replaced by monetary payments. German historians emphasise the part played by the Germans in this medieval colonisation, as if the genius of the German settler were the cause of the whole process. In reality this process was caused by economic conditions, which naturally brought foreign nationals to the

The Tombstone of King Přemysl Otakar II
St. Vitus' Cathedral, Prague, A. D. 1375—78

country. But the Czech landowners soon perceived the advantage of founding villages in the new way and in course of time they gave the advantages of the "German right" to old villages too. The fact that the initiator of colonisation of the Eastern Moravian lands was Bishop Robert the Englishman, whom we have mentioned above, testifies that the process was not a German affair.

The colonisation was increased by external stimulus as well. From the centre of Asia the Tartar armies started their march to Europe. The Russian principalities tried to defend the gates of Europe but they did not succeed. The Tartar flood poured into Poland and in 1241 reached Central Europe. The King of Hungary was routed by the Tartars and the same befell the Piast Princes of Silesia. There was some truth in the sentence written a little later by a Czech author: "We are your wall against the pagan nations, and if we succumb, and our house is ruined, you will be threatened by danger and ruin too." Certainly there were other reasons for the Tartar withdrawal to the East and South, but the fact that in front of the mountain-gates of Bohemia the Tartars turned back gave Bohemia the title of the "shield of Europe." Eastern Moravia and Slovakia were not spared from terrible devastation. Whole regions were depopulated, the process of colonisation was accelerated, and a ring of castles grew up throughout the country. The castles were not only permanent fortresses but the economic centres of the estates and potential centres of regional administration.

Přemysl Otakar II, the son of Wenceslas, took over a kingdom internally united, economically prosperous, and culturally flourishing. By his marriage with the Austrian ducal house of Babenberg, he secured for himself the passages through the Alps and the routes along the Danube. He won public opinion by his crusades against the Prussians, and finally engaged in combat with the Hungarian king Bela in a fight for Central Europe. In 1260 he won the Battle of Kressenbrunn and incorporated the countries of the Alps with his kingdom, in this way becoming the sovereign of the most powerful state in Central Europe. The "King of Gold and Iron", as he was called for his military and economic power, became an ally of the English prince Richard of Cornwall, the German King-Elect. Richard gave the King of Bohemia the title of "Protector of the Imperial Property on the Right Bank of the Rhine," he confirmed his conquests and indirectly supported

Přemysl when he acquired new dominions comprising the city of Cheb, Carinthia and even some regions in Italy. Přemysl's second marriage to the grand-daughter of the King of Hungary and the temporary occupation of western Slovakia seem to indicate his intention to develop the Czech state in a south-eastern direction. But there was another plan, even more tempting. Přemysl was the first King of Bohemia to be able to take advantage of the position of his State in relation to Germany, and began to lay claim to the imperial crown. At that time there was no power in Germany which could oppose his ambitious plans, but the Papal Curia interfered, being afraid of a strong Emperor. After the death of Richard of Cornwall, an unknown Swiss Count, Rudolf of Hapsburg, became King of Germany. Twice Přemysl tried to alter destiny; at the second attempt he fell in the battle of Marchfeld in 1278.

The great personality of this King of Bohemia brought for the first time a Czech layman into European literature. Dante and Grillparzer, English and Spanish dramatists were captivated by his tragic end. The reasons for King Otakar's good fortune and tragic end lay, above all, in Bohemia itself. King Přemysl was overcome in a struggle in which Czech nobility was his most dangerous opponent. This new social class was just gaining unusual power, thanks to its right to decide the height of an extraordinary tax which was becoming the real source of the State's income. Of course it did not yield the taxes for nothing. The advantages the aristocrats gained gradually gave birth to a Court of Justice and a Diet for the country. Přemysl tried to win the support of a new social stratum, which was the cities. Essentially, cities were those communities that were granted the privilege of holding markets and having a judge and a priest, in fact self-administration. The cities were subject to the King through the medium of his officers, they were king's fortresses and sources of new income. Most of them had their origin in settlements of newcomers, very often on the sites of old market-villages. Frequently the foreign, German element remained limited to patricians. Only those cities which were constantly strengthened by a flow from German provinces or which formed a part of continuous German territory held out against the subsequent Czech counter-attack.

However it would be wrong to think that Přemysl was as a sovereign a stranger to his people. At his court German propagandists had their place side by side with the Italian lawyers, who planned the codification of the laws of the country and directed a School of Law which Přemysl intended to change into a university. Out of this international milieu came the so-called "Letter to Poland", probably composed by one of the pupils of the Master of Rhetoric, the Italian Henry of Isernia. It was an eloquent appeal in a time full of danger, complaining against the insatiable ambition of the Germans, an ambition which left to develop unchecked would not be satisfied with the enslavement of the Czechs but would mean the end of a free Poland as well.

During the five years after the Battle of Marchfeld, the German Margrave, Otto of Brandenburg, ruled in Bohemia. The little son of Přemysl II was kept a prisoner in Germany and a Hapsburg sovereign was appointed for Moravia. But this German occupation, the first German Protectorate, met with resistance from the Czech nobility, clergy and people. For the first time in Czech history the feudal community gained a success with the enthronement of Wenceslas II. As the new sovereign married a Hapsburg princess, expansion to the south was closed to him, therefore his attention turned to the Slavonic East. After three centuries the Czech king re-united under his sceptre Bohemia and Poland. The mighty Czech-Polish bloc became increased by Hungary at the beginning of the next century. A part of the Hungarian nobility, especially that coming from present-day Slovakia, offered the crown of St. Stephen to Wenceslas' little son. The old rivals soon opposed this bloc with an armed resistance. The Hapsburg King of Germany and the Pope did their best to destroy the unity of the Přemyslid State. It was not easy, as Wenceslas II had at his disposal the great economic strength of a country, the "California" of the Middle Ages. Nearly at the same time mining towns in Bohemia and Slovakia became prosperous. Wenceslas II used the riches in ore for a reform of the coinage and the organisation of mining industry. The "groschen" of Prague, on the model of the French coins of Louis IX, were minted at Kutná Hora by specialists from Florence. They and the Hungarian ducats from Kremnica belonged to the currency most in demand in the Middle Ages. Bohemian mining law not only spread to Hungary and farther East, but was considered so exemplary that three centuries later Sir Philip Sidney wanted to introduce it in the American Colonies. In the end an unhappy accident or invidious fate helped the enemies of the Czech kingdom. The health of Wenceslas II, undermined in his youth, suddenly broke down in the year 1305, and a year later the young king Wenceslas III was killed at Olomouc by an unknown murderer. The united kingdom of the Přemyslids collapsed with the dying out of the dynasty.

But the work of the Přemyslids was not wholly destroyed. The Czech State was again restricted to Bohemia and Moravia alone, but the economic foundation and the cultural achievement of the Czech nation remained. The national awareness of the Czechs found expression in Latin Annals and in the first Czech rhymed chronicle, The Chronicle of Dalimil. A century of unbroken growth created in the country new social divisions, a proud aristocracy, a rich clergy, prosperous burghers and half-free peasants. The aristocracy was a national-minded one, although it had been formed scarcely two centuries before under foreign influence and bearing German names. The growth of the fine arts gave the first indication of their future riches, to which not only Germany but Byzantium, France and Italy were to contribute. The fusion of foreign cultures with the Czech milieu found its flowering in the conception of a Czech national spirit and moreover in the broader Slav consciousness, growing out of a kinship of language and common interests.

IV

THE AGE OF THE LUXEMBURGS

The great nations of Western Europe never had to concentrate all their energies on self-preservation as in nearly all generations the smaller Slavonic nations did. The crisis which the Czechs underwent after 1306 was not fatal only because it came after a period of national expansion, and because it was followed by a period of national reaction. When in 1310 the youthful John of Luxemburg ascended the throne of Bohemia, Czech nationalism had the opportunity to get to know the spiritual movements then flourishing in Western Europe.

The dynasty of which John was an offspring was closely connected with France, at that time the most powerful state in Europe and the seat of international Papacy. Paris and Avignon became sources of spiritual currents influencing Prague, which in turn interpreted these influences to Central Europe. The Czech Gothic was so living that it lasted till the 17th century, to be followed in church architecture immediately by Baroque. Direct contact with France put an end to the dominating influence of the German intermediary. It was followed by the cultural rapprochement with the West, and marked the beginning of Czech "Europeanism". The apostles of this "Europeanism" were Czech students visiting Bologna, Paris, Oxford and Cambridge; pilgrims wandering to Rome, Compostella and Canterbury; clergy called to Avignon; and nobles fascinated by the courts of western Europe.

The adventurous King John who had a finger in all the major intrigues of contemporary Europe did not lack a clear political plan. This monarch, to whom tradition gave the nickname of the "Foreign King", strengthened the Czech State with the acquisition of a greater part of Silesia and Upper Lusatia, and his influence was felt in Slo-

A Bust of King John of Bohemia
St. Vitus' Cathedral, Prague, A. D. 1375—78

vakia. Without doubt his political aim was the creation of a power which for the eastern region of the medieval Roman Empire would fulfill the role of France. During his lifetime the Prague Bishopric was transformed under the benevolence of the Pope into an Archbishopric, so that even in the ecclesiastical field the last trace of German dependence disappeared.

The crowning success of John's diplomacy was the election of his son Charles to the German throne. When in 1346 John was killed on the battlefield of Crécy, fighting against the English Black Prince, his death could not destroy his political achievement. Although he was an enemy, the bravery of such a death made an unforgettable impression on the English. His work was brought to completion by Charles IV, a monarch at once wise and happy. He was at the same time Slav and Westerner, for in his education he was French and through his mother and his own sympathies he was Czech.

With the help of the Papal Curia, he was able to transform Bohemia into the centre of the medieval empire, endowed with many privileges, and thus he realised the plans of his great-grandfather, Přemysl II. Although wounded at Crécy and on more than occasion in his life manifesting unusual courage, he did not like war. His pacifism earned him the nickname of the "Popish King". For in those times war was the normal activity of feudal lords.

But certainly his policy was justified by its success. Without fighting he acquired the rest of Silesia and Lusatia, and created an entity which survived as the "Crown of Bohemia" until the Thirty Years' War. Brandenburg, with its second Electoral vote, was acquired by him, and Berlin became a provincial outpost of the Czech State. He secured expansion further to the East, where his son Sigismund became King of Hungary, and to the West, where Luxemburg was inherited by his first-born son, Wenceslas. Towards the end of the 14th century the Luxemburgs had no rivals in Europe, because their dominions extended from the Adriatic to the Baltic, and from Luxemburg to Hungary. The monarch and his court were in every sense of the word international. Charles himself more than once called himself the "heir of the Great Moravian Empire". In a letter addressed to the King of Serbia, he laid stress on his Slavonic origin. He founded a monastery in Prague for monks of Slavonic liturgy, and this monastery was soon called "The Slavonic". By his cultural activities he gave a model to the King

King Charles IV

A detail from a votive picture of Jan Očko of Vlašim, A. D. 1373

of Poland, and in the West he tried to spread the knowledge of Slavonic Saints.

Charles IV, like other great men of the Czech nation, stands between East and West of Europe as a tolerant and pacifist citizen of the European orbit. In fact, he was even asked to mediate between England and France, and her ally, Scotland. But his feet were on firm ground. He cared as much for the introduction of a new vine from Burgundy or a new species of plum as for the erection of a new Cathedral at the hands of Master Matthew of Arras. He was a great town-planner and under his direction Prague became a modern town, much larger than contemporary London or Paris. Even more, Prague became the seat of the first university north of the Alps. The monarch, whose realism led him to reject the far-flung plans of Cola di Rienzo and Francesco Petrarca, became an inspired founder of a University. This University was created on the model of the Sorbonne, "so that the Czechs did not need to beg for the crumbs of learning abroad, but found at home a laden table". The internationalism of this university gradually declined, but it remained a centre of learning for the Czech lands and Slovakia. When in 1409 the Czech masters got control of the University, the Prague centre of learning was already appropriated for the Czechs.

During Charles's reign humanism reached the country in different ways. Elsewhere, humanism reached the people through the medium of court, church and nobility. It was not so in Bohemia. Charles's court of Prague was international, and individual clergy and nobility were too much under the influence of that spirit. Another generation would have been needed to bring humanist ideas to the people. If the people nevertheless got something of the riches of humanism, especially its practical Christian philosophy, it was thanks to the effort of a new Czech intelligentsia, mostly clergy sprung from the people.

And so we find a humanist conception of common weal in Charles's attempt to codify the laws of the country, in Archbishop Ernest's attempt to put an end to ordeals and duels and in the works of theologians and preachers. The Czech humanism was soon diverted to the field of morals and religion, and the interest in learning and the pagan joy of life disppeared into the background.

This attachment to criticism of morals was a specific reaction to the contemporary decline of morality. The Czech intellectual witnessed the worldliness of the clergy under the protection of the Emperor,

Queen Anne of Bohemia
From an old English print

the well-being of foreigners and the misery of the people. He came to the conclusion that mankind was living badly, and that the Church needed reform. One of the precursors of the Czech religious reformation, Master Matthias of Janov, compared the life of his contemporaries with that of the first Christians and came to the conclusion "that the lord is for the community and not the community for the lord". The yeoman, Thomas Štítný, the first layman to write on religion, went even farther and said, "that in the beginning there were no lords and there was equality among the people." The idea of a common weal taking care of the "good ploughman" as well as of the landlord was able to shake the social pyramid of the later Middle Ages.

When the seed-time had come, there appeared the founder of the Czech Reformation. Master John Hus was the son of the South Bohemian countryside, who became a preacher in the Chapel of Bethlehem, founded in Prague for the popular classes. He was a learned man, Rector of the University. He was the author of a reform of orthography, which gave the Czech language its present graphic appearance, and even influenced other Slavonic and non-Slavonic languages. Science and life were united in his activity. He was influenced by the older tradition, possibly an outcome of the teaching of the South French sect of the Waldenses. But especially he was influenced by the reformed ideas of the Oxford master, John Wycliffe. The twentieth century has little feeling for the subtle dogmatic differences of the medieval pamphlets, but the teaching of Hus and Wycliffe, that divine law was laid down by the Bible, was an entirely new idea to the European mind. The authority of Church and State was confronted with the idea of divine inspiration, and the conscience of the individual. Hus's often quoted sentence, that "it is better to obey God than the people", sealed at last by the death of the reformer, belongs to the triumphs of the human mind.

Wycliffe, whose choice was a quiet end at Lutterworth, was overshadowed by the steadfastness of Hus, and Luther's weakness for authoritarianism and compromising contrasts with Hus's passionate appeal to the individual. Hence the Czech Hussite movement is independent enough not to be taken merely as a prologue to the German Reformation.

Hus's criticism of the clergy led to a conflict with the Church, and the Council of Constance sentenced Hus as a heretic, because he was not willing to abandon his belief until persuaded of his error. His judges, nearly all followers of the humanist enlightenment, probably did not realise that they were sentencing a man whose humanism reached a farther logical conclusion than their own. The authority of the Council refused to persuade the reformer, who chose to die at the stake, on the 6th of July, 1415. Next year he was followed by his friend, Master Jerome of Prague. As a student Jerome wandered to England, whose queen was the Bohemian princess, Anne, and from there he brought back the writings of Wycliffe. Italian humanists, who witnessed the heretic's end, had to admire his courage.

At the same time as the English Lollards were being crushed by Henry V, the death of Hus gave an impetus to a great revolution in Bohemia. The Czechs did not believe that Hus was a heretic, and did not care. They were especially outraged that the Emperor broke his pledge of safe-conduct, given to Hus. The death of Hus was for the Czechs an insult to their "most Christian kingdom", and the nobility of Bohemia and Moravia declared in their manifesto that John Hus was a good, just and Christian man, the pride of Bohemia and of the Slavonic language, and that his teaching would be defended with the sword.

V

THE HUSSITE AGE OF ENLIGHTENMENT

The age of Charles IV, like many great epochs in history was an era of transition. On the one hand it brought the fruits of the political and cultural growth of the precedent times, on the other hand it contained the seeds of the coming storms in the social and spiritual spheres. The reign of Charles' successor, Wenceslas IV, is marked by the life and activity of Master John Hus. Wenceslas had neither Henry V's inclination to break heresy at home, nor his power and prestige. In the prolonged struggle between higher and lower nobility he took the side of the socially lower class, from which he chose his advisors. In quieter days his court would most probably have become the centre of national culture, in stormy times it collapsed in the end, just as the political power of the Luxemburgs did.

Wenceslas IV died at a time when crowds of preachers, freely delivering sermons on the Gospel and predicting the nearing end of the world, were going up and down the country. At the same time the lower nobility began to look greedily upon the property of rich orders and churches, peasants began to hope for the easing of the heavy rents due to their landlords, and the people in workshops and suburbs began to rise against the patricians of a foreign language. The death of Hus gave his teaching a national character, and elements of social revolt began to attach themselves to the religious and national revolution. And because the heir of Wenceslas was his brother, that Emperor Sigismund who broke his pledge at Constance and showed no willingness to negotiate with the rebels, the pressure of fear transformed the religious enthusiasts to a set of revolutionary fanatics.

"The old world is dying and is drawing to its close", wrote the

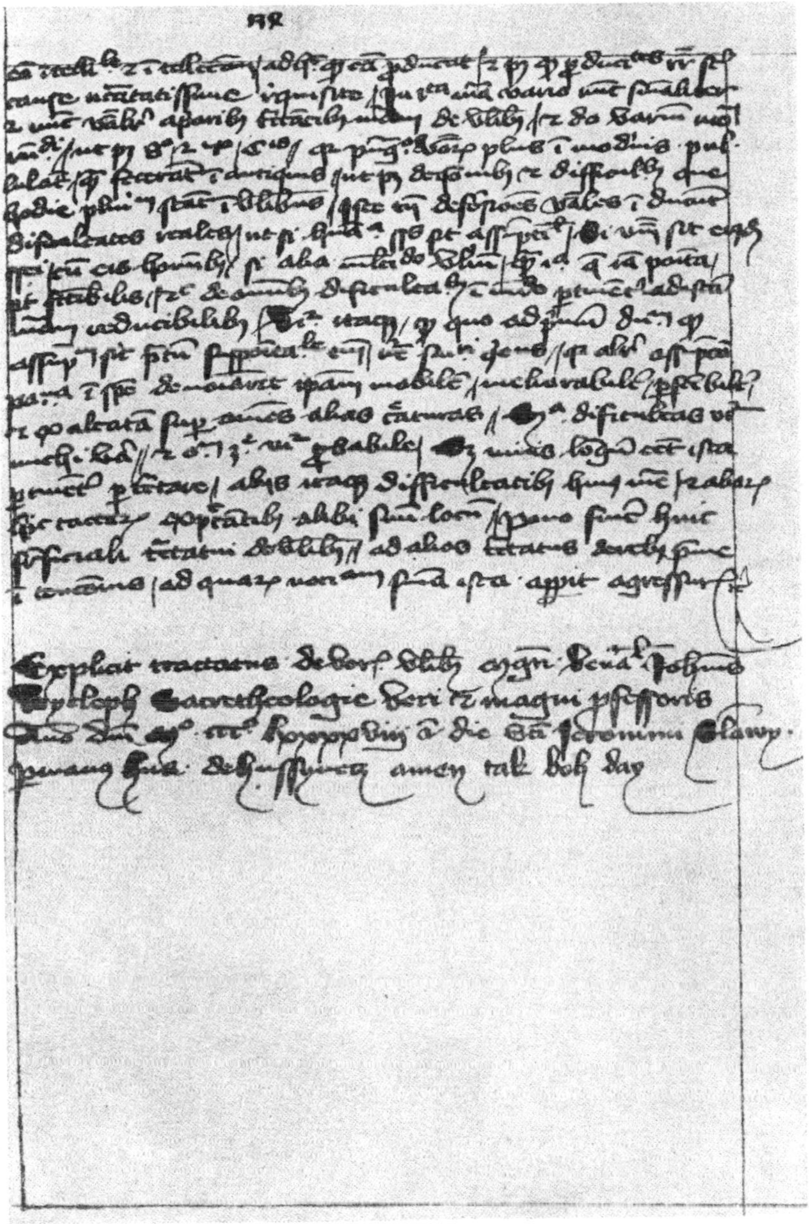

Jan Hus' Transcript of a Wycliffe's Treatise

The National Library, Prague

Masters of the University of Prague. "The reign of sin will end with the arrival of Christ", said the popular preachers. Then "kings, princes and prelates will disappear . . . the oppression of the poor will come to an end ...there will be neither kings nor officials, because the Law of God will be inscribed in all hearts". This mood of chiliasm and anarchy caused the burning down of castles and monasteries, and the flood of destruction threatened to ruin the cultural achievement of preceding ages.

But as the end of the world did not appear, the real danger proved to be the Emperor's crusade. The followers of Hus turned into God's Warriors. Upon the banks of the river Lužnice a new town arose with the biblical name of Tábor. Its inhabitants proclaimed in the spirit of Christian communism that nobody should have his own property, but that all should own everything in common. The brethren and sisters of Tábor, mostly tradesmen and peasants, were supported by members of the lower nobility, who had in the meantime seized the churchproperty and were fighting the all-powerful barons. The Taborites found allies in the city of Prague and its University.

In 1420 Prague became the goal of a great crusade consisting of Germans, French, Italians, Hungarians, Austrians and even some Englishmen. At the height of the danger, the community of Tábor came to help the besieged Prague. The army of Taborites was led by John Žižka, a country squire who had once helped the Poles to break the power of the Teutonic Knights. It managed to repulse the flower of European chivalry from the Czech capital, and this made the drawing up of the Hussite programme possible.

The citizens of Prague, the lower nobility and the brethren and sisters of Tábor agreed in the so-called Four Articles of Prague 1. to support the free preaching of the Gospel, 2. that the sacrament of the Holy Eucharist should be administered in both kinds, 3. to put an end to the possession of worldly goods by the clergy, 4. to insist on the punishment of mortal sins even of the members of the clergy. Such was the programme among the authors of which was Wycliffe's pupil Master Peter the Englishman.

It was impossible to defeat the united Hussites. The crusaders were defeated in front of Prague, at the foot of the hill of Vítkov, renamed Žižkov, and a second time beneath Vyšehrad, once the royal seat. In 1421 the crusaders fled from the Western Bohemian town of Žatec

Jan Hus at the Stake
The Codex of Jena, 2nd half of 15th c.

without even seeing the Hussites. In the following year Žižka put the crusaders to flight near Kutná Hora. There, at the outbreak of the Hussite revolution, the German citizens threw thousands of Czech heretics into the mines. The fighting spirit of the Hussites, of which the song "Ye, Warriors of God" became the literary expression, was slowly attaining legendary fame. It derived its strength from the religious exaltation of God's Warriors, and also from the military efficiency of the lower nobility, which had been driven into foreign service since the 14th century by lack of means.

The genius of Žižka provided the Hussites with a strong military organisation, and transformed the Hussite troops into a disciplined infantry, whose weaknesses became an advantage by suitable choice of arms, mostly converted peasants' tools. The feudal cavalry had no chance against light, well equipped infantry, skilfully using the advantages of terrain and protected by a barricade of heavy waggons and a shower of arrows and shots. Czech howitzers and waggon-barricades triumphed over the cunning Italian condottieri, cardinals and even over the English Prince Henry of Beaufort, Bishop of Winchester.

After Žižka's death the cleric Procopius the Bald took over the leadership and the Hussite defence was changed into an offensive. The Hussite raids, followed by a propaganda campaign of pamphlets, brought unrest into the neighbouring countries and took the Hussites as far as the shores of the Baltic. In vain did Joan of Arc threaten from France that she would set out against the heretics, in vain did the pope issue bulls of damnation. In 1431 the last crusade was dispersed near Domažlice and there was nobody left in Europe, who would take upon himself the burden of a hopeless expedition. On the contrary, Czech howitzers and Czech captains were often invited to other countries in order to employ their military craft.

The victories and the raids of the Hussites brought, however, into their ranks many for whom pillage meant more than religious belief. There were many in the country who longed for peace and for the end of destruction and slaughter. In Southern Bohemia the thinker Peter Chelčický preached on the text of the Commandment: Thou shalt not kill. He emphasized the need for a return to the religion of primitive Christianity, free from "pagan additions", and attacked the contemporary love of conquest. His ideal of Christian reform became the inspiration for the founders of the Unity of Brethren.

Church of St. Martin-in-the-Wall
Prague, 1st half of 12th c., rebuilt in the 2nd half of 14th c.

The ecclesiastical council summoned to meet at Basle in Switzerland accepted the principle, for which Master John Hus had died; that the Holy Scriptures should be the final judge in the disputes between Czechs and Church. The Taborites, who became the spokesmen of the militant group, were forced to yield to the desire of the majority for peace, when they were defeated in the fratricidal battle of Lipany in 1434.

Then nothing stood in the way of reconciliation of the Czechs and the Council. The Four Articles of Prague were accepted as the basis for the Compacts of Basle. By these, the Czechs were allowed to use the communion cup, from now on the common symbol of all the utraquists. The religious reconciliation was followed by political. The old Emperor Sigismund acknowledged the Compacts and was accepted as king.

Such was the end of the first, the heroic period of the Hussite revolution. What were its results for the nation? This revolution of small people brought material advantage mostly to the nobles, who seized the property of the Crown and the Church. The loss of royal lands undermined the royal power economically, so that it lay at the mercy of the nobility. The clergy, once an ally of the Crown, lost its influence and ceased to be a political force. In this, the case of Bohemia was exceptional in the West of Europe. Cities became the rivals of the nobility, remaining divided into higher and lower ranks. Prague specially gained a great deal of power and esteem, so that foreign observers compared it to the republic of Venice. The peasants suffered from the effects of the long drawn-out wars and found themselves after their conclusion more than ever bound to the soil. This class of people which had made the greatest sacrifice to the Hussite cause gained nothing from it materially in the end.

The development of the Czech nation and culture was, no doubt, quickened by the revolution. But just as the Catholics retained their position in the border districts, the German population remained in those areas as well. The Czech language took the lead in the literary life of the country, especially in religious aspects of it, and was bringing enlightenment among the people. Towards the middle of the 15th century the courteous Italian ecclesiastic magnate, Aeneas Sylvius, better known as Pope Pius II, had to admit, that the Hussite women knew the Scriptures better than Italian bishops and that, on the whole

lawowo tielo h[illegible]edano bylo / wzaw yy zlatych gewra
til. A teprúw nossenije podle obyčege učiniwsse sp/
rawedlíwy kraali pohzeb dokonali
¶ O Janowi Žižkowi Czeskee roty Haytmanu wo/
denij preudatneem a przewijtieznee, Kap xxxviij

¶ Ecce fflagellum dei

n Edawno vmrzel Watzlaw kdyz Jan Žižka
rodu Vrozeneeho z mijsta kteremuž Tross/
now gmeeno gest Platu maleho / na Dwo/
rze kralowskeem od detinstwije wychowany a w Bo/
giich wyzwiženy gednoho nemage oka kterez vdatne
boyuge giz przed tijm ztratil pilen gsa Husowa vče
nije a lúpežij žadostiw / sebraw obecžneho lidu Woy

Jan Žižka of Trocnov at the Front of His Troops
A wood-carving from Mikuláš Konáč's translation of Historia Bohemica by Eneo Silvio Piccolomini, A. D. 1510

"this wicked people has one good quality – namely that it is fond of learning".

Religious feeling became the characteristics of the Czech nation. The rise in the standard of education, of purely medieval character of course, was paid by the spiritual isolation of the Hussite Bohemia, and by the one-sided emphasis on religious matters. The political consequences of the fact that the Hussites failed to take firm hand of all the country were also serious. Unfortunately, the Hussites never mastered Moravia, Silesia and Lusatia, so that the core of the Czech state was reduced to its extent of the 12th century Bohemia. Besides, the devastation of some Czech territories and the decrease of the population led to the revival of the German colonisation of the border regions.

The Hussite movement which brought the Czechs temporarily in the foreground of European politics was therefore dearly bought. The Czech reform came too soon to meet with a response in the rest of Europe, which only a century later showed a more favourable attitude towards Luther. The results of the revolution in the national field were most positive, because the Hussite military impetus paved the way for the expansion of the Czech language, taking place in the next period.

The Hussite movement returned consciously to the Slavonic traditions, cherished by Charles IV. In their manifestos the Hussites stressed the solidarity of Slavonic nations. Following the example of Great Moravia they too sent messengers to Constantinople, the cradle of the Orthodox Church. Peter the Englishman was the leader of this mission.

One cannot overlook the influence of the Hussite revolution on the development of European society. For this it was, especially in its early, radical form, a powerful shock. The echo of this shock had to be suppressed especially in the neighbouring Germany. Finally, it accelerated the disorganisation of the medieval feudal society and its change into the society directed by the Estates. The greatest asset of the Hussite revolution, without doubt, lies in its contribution to the history of the European spirit, in its uncompromising faith in the importance of every individual's free thought, without which human progress is unthinkable. Of all the fruits of the Czech reform, this faith in Man speaks to the present day in the most comprehensible language.

VI

ON THE THRESHOLD OF THE NEW TIMES

The time following the recognition of King Sigismund meant only defence for the Hussite movement for a time. The Turkish danger began to threaten more clamorously, and when Sigismund died in 1437, it was the fear of that very danger that led the Estates of the Alpine lands (Austria), of Hungary and of Bohemia to elect a common king for the first time in history. He was Albert of Habsburg, the husband of Sigismund's daughter, Elizabeth of Luxemburg. In Bohemia the election of Albert was not unanimous – the party of radical Hussites supported the candidature of the Polish king, related to the country by language, and only the early death of Albert prevented a civil war. The Hussite party was then driven into defence and therefore the claims of the widow Elizabeth of Luxemburg and her son, Ladislaus Posthumus, were recognised in the end. The Bohemian-Austro-Hungarian union, however, fell to pieces after Albert's death. A majority of Hungarian noblemen chose for their sovereign the Polish king Vladislav, and only the northern part of the country, the old Upper Hungary (the Upper Country), roughly corresponding to the present Slovakia, remained faithful to Elizabeth, whose power here rested on the troops of Czech captains (hejtmans) led by John Jiskra of Brandýs. Although the Czech captains were mostly Catholics, the majority of their soldiers were Hussites and the times of the Czech "Brotherhood" became an important era in the evolution of Slovakia, which again attained a significant position with regard to public law and home rule within the framework of the Hungarian crown – and that happened at a time when the Czech cultural influence could fully develop in the country.

When in 1444 the Polish king Vladislav died, in a battle against the Turks near the Bulgarian Varna, Hungary continued to remain separated into two "countries" – the Lower, led by the Governor John Hunyady, and the Upper, led by Jiskra. The young George of Poděbrady, the leader of the Hussite party, was coming to a similar position towards the forties of the century in Bohemia. George came from a noble family, which had sacrificed much in the Utraquist struggle. As a fourteen year old boy he saw in the battle of Lipany a warning example of the results of a split in the nation; he went through a political school of provincial meetings and assemblies, always fighting for the Hussite rights against the leaders of the Catholic nobility, who became overbearing, thanks to the King's support. In 1448 George captured Prague, when the danger of a Catholic reaction was looming on the horizon. From the leader of a single party he became administrator of the whole kingdom of Bohemia, and defended the unity of the kingdom so successfully, that he gained the respect of Aeneas Sylvius, whom he met towards the beginning of the fifties at the Hussite Tábor. He became Regent for the infant Ladislaus Posthumus, and was able to re-establish peace, order and righteousness so quickly that the years of the "Beardless King", i. e. of George's administration, remained for centuries the golden age of Czech economic life.

In 1457 Ladislaus Posthumus died a victim of one of those diseases, which made the life of medieval man so uncertain. His death took place just before he was to have married a French princess. The chronicler from Silesian Wratislavia described the scene in which the young dying king bequeathed the Bohemian and Hungarian kingdom to George's care. The Bohemian nobles really chose George as their king, and many people cried for joy that merciful God had liberated them from the power of German rulers. By George's influence the young son of Hunyady, Matthias Corvinus, the husband of George's daughter, became King of Hungary. In George the representative of the second Hussite generation ascended the throne, those for whom the ideals of the Hussite revolution were not empty words but who succeeded in combining the security of the Hussite inheritance with the interests of the nation as a whole. The Hussite king, whose goal was peace and order, was, in the meantime, king of two peoples, sovereign of both Hussite and Catholic subjects, and he did not hesitate to try to bring about reconciliation between both parties in the kingdom. A statue

A View of London
A copper-plate by Václav Hollar

of him holding a sword in his hand was placed on the front of the Týn Church in Prague, above the communion-cup and the motto, God's Truth Prevails – yet among his friends and advisers were a considerable number of his Catholic subjects. And on his estate in Eastern Bohemia the founders of the Czech Unity of Brethren found a safe refuge.

In a short time George restored the royal authority in Bohemia, Moravia, Silesia and also in Lusatia. The old Bohemian state was restored. Neighbouring rulers were not slow to establish relations with the Hussite King, who was even called in to decide in dynastic differences in the neighbourhood. Even George's German subjects seemed to come to life again along with their Czech fellow-citizens. Besides the idea of arbitration and universal peace, another thought occupied George's mind. The Turkish question was becoming steadily more acute, as Turkish territory was spreading in the Balkans. George was evidently ready to use Czech military power in the struggle against the Turks. The Turkish danger motivated his suggestion of establishing a League of Christian Princes from the year 1462. This plan, the author of which was George's humanist diplomat, Antoine Marini of Grenoble, was built on the universalist basis of the political thinking of the Renaissance, and had purely practical aims as well. At the time when George was sending messengers to France to realise his plan, he was being badly oppressed by the papal court which intended to force him to sacrifice his Hussite faith. George was determined not to do this and so in 1462 Pius II, an old acquaintance of the Hussite king, solemnly denied the validity of the Basle Compacts. The League of European Princes was directed against the Pope as well as against the Turks, because it saw no place for the Roman Curia in the secular organisation of Europe. It was effective: the Pope retreated for a time, became reconciled even with the King of France, Louis XI – the prime partner of George in this diplomatic play, the outcome of which was a treaty of Franco-Bohemian alliance, which saved the Hussite Czechs from political isolation.

When, after the death of Pius II the struggle between the Bohemians and the papal court broke out openly, there was no ruler among the neighbours of the Czech heretics who would have been willing to lead the crusade. The flag of rebellion was carried by the German citizens of the Silesian Wratislavia, supported by the treacherous son-in-law of the Bohemian king, Matthias Corvinus, who preferred the fight for the growth of his own power to the less magnificent struggle against the Turks. The strife had just turned to the disadvantage of the Hungarian king when in the year 1471 George suddenly died. His political inheritance did not die with him, even when, for a time, Matthias usurped the rule over Moravia, Silesia and Lusatia. The struggle in which George, according to his own words, engaged not for the sake of war, but for the sake of peace, ended with the enthronement of King Vladislav of the Polish family of Jagellon, which had been prepared for by George. After the death of Matthias Vladislav became his heir in Hungary too (1490), so that the countries of the Bohemian crown were again united, and, further, the Slovak part of Hungary was connected especially with the neighbouring Moravia through newly-established relations.

If George's pacifism did not remain fruitless, his efforts to free politics from the influence of religion penetrated even among his Catholic subjects. The Catholic John of Rabštejn declared that he did not think that "secular and church affairs should be united" and, in advance of his times, asked that "both should remain in their respective domains, not standing in each other's way, not damaging each other". This secularisation of thinking among the broad classes in Bohemia, which we can follow from the time of George in Czech literature as well, helped to prepare the way for religious toleration.

The time of George's followers, Vladislav of Jagellon and his son Louis is, therefore, an era of common Czecho-Hungarian political life, the reason for which was the growing Turkish danger, and which had beneficial results in the establishing of relations between the Czech countries and the present Slovakia. The Czech language began, at the same time, its expansion to Poland, ruled by other members of the Jagellon dynasty. At this time Czech influence is recognisable even further to the East in Hungary, in the Roumanian Multania, and even in Russia – usually in connection with the activity of adherents to some Hussite sect, who brought into these countries the revolutionary idea of translating Holy Writ, the highest judge in matters of faith, into the language of the people. If we add to this the renewed Czech cultural efforts, the establishing of new relations with the West and, finally, the development of plastic, painting and graphic arts, connected with the so-called Vladislav style, in reality late Gothic, corresponding to the Plateresque style in contemporary Spain and the Tudor style in England, we must acknowledge the cultural significance of the political efforts of the second Hussite generation.

Nothing illustrates the greatness of the Czech spirit in the 15th century more clearly than the fact that the religious revolution led, in the end, to the recognition of the ideal of religious toleration. In 1485, representatives of the Bohemian Estates met at Kutná Hora and made the following declaration about religion: "Item, with regard to the Catholic and the Utraquist churches, no party will in the future be allowed to suppress the other, neither in secular, nor in spiritual matters, and both should have sympathy for each other. Priests of both parties... will freely preach the Gospel... none of them will call the other heretic, and dukes, lords and knights and royal towns will not oppress their subjects because of their faith... nor oppose their achieving salvation according to their customs and their creed."

In the religious peace of Kutná Hora medieval Bohemia anticipated the Edict of Nantes by a whole century and became the first country in Europe where religious toleration was guaranteed by law.

VII

"THE GOLDEN ERA OF BOHEMIA"

In 1526 Louis of Jagellon, King of Bohemia and Hungary, fell in the Battle of Mohacs. The orphaned kingdom, directly threatened by the Turks, who three years later pushed through as far as Vienna, for the third time in its history chose for king a member of the Habsburg family, who could unite the Austrian, Hungarian and Czech countries into a powerful Central European federation. He was Ferdinand I, the husband of Ann, a Jagellon Princess. The Hapsburg dynasty was then at the height of its power; Ferdinand's brother Charles V was reigning over the Spanish Empire, over which already the sun never set, with which magnificent India and America were linked, and he was, besides, Emperor of the Holy Roman Empire and ruler of the rich Netherlands – and an ally of Henry VIII. Ferdinand was esteemed by the Czech Hussites to be an especially suitable ruler to settle the old struggle between the Czechs and Rome.

Very soon, however, internal discord arose between the Estates and the new sovereign. First, the differences were of a constitutional character. Ferdinand, who had been brought up in Spain, was not willing to allow the Estates to behave in accordance with the privileges which they had gained in the time of the Hussite revolution. The relations between King and nation were complicated by the quarrels of religious origin in neighbouring Germany. During the first years of the Hapsburg reign in Bohemia, Luther's movement was gaining ground in large parts of Germany. Lutheranism, however, did not become the religion of all Germany, just as Hussitism did not gain all Bohemia. What was still worse was the fact that Luther entrusted the German dukes, who cared little for the freedom of thought of their subjects, with provincial church administration. While the Hapsburgs, after an initial hesitation, stood against the reform, the Czech Hussites were gradually won over to its side. The Czechs, who in the beginning of the 16th century called themselves "faithful sons of the church", became under the influence of Lutheranism radical partisans of Lutheran reform. That is why Ferdinand I was not successful when he obtained permission from the Pope for the Czechs to use the communion-cup. Even then the Czech Utraquists were in reality – if not yet in name – Lutherans. When in 1547 open conflict broke out in Germany between Charles V and adherents to Lutheranism, the Czechs stood on the side opposed to the Hapsburgs. An open conflict did not break out in Bohemia, but the Czechs paid for the lost struggle. Because the aristocracy made haste to humiliate before the monarch, the resistance against the king was paid for by the followers of the Unity of Brethren and especially the royal burghs or free towns whose old economic and administrative privileges were chopped off to such a degree that they ceased to exist as a political factor. In this first struggle between the idea of religious and political freedom and the idea of Catholic and royal authority, the Czechs were deprived of many a fruit of their own spiritual evolution. The king, who was persecuting the followers of the Czech Unity of Brethren, then only just beginning to lay the foundations of its influence upon Czech culture, had, certainly, no understanding of the words with which John of Perštejn turned to him in 1539: "Faith is a gift of God, and he, to whom it was not given by God, cannot receive it from people." The Czech and Moravian noblemen, even though they shortsightedly let the Czech Brethren and the citizens pay for their safety, were more inclined to fight than to "suffer violence on their conscience".

Tension continued between king and Estates, ceasing only in 1564 with Ferdinand's death. His son, Maximilian II, was well-known for his sympathies to the idea of religious reform. Even though for family reasons he never went over to the Lutherans, he never persecuted anybody in his country for his faith. Thus the complete change of Hussitism under the Lutheran reformation, the new growth of the Czech Union of Brethren, was made possible and thus too the foundations of appeasement and calm were laid. The reign of Maximilian is noteworthy for the success of the struggle against the Turks, for with abundant Czech assistance the frontier of Hapsburg Hungary, which

The Belvedere in Prague
By Paolo della Stella and Bonifác Wohlmuth,
A. D. 1535—63

in the north corresponded closely to the contemporary Czechoslovak-Hungarian frontier, was fixed. The tension between the nobility and the dynasty ceased. Cultural relations with the rest of Europe, especially with the West, were re-established. Czech students left in great numbers for Italy, France and also for Spain and England. The peace resulted also in economic growth, for it was possible to export a considerable surplus of economic products to foreign countries. This "Golden era of Czech towns" had, however, its less glorious aspects. The country continued to be pursued by the curse of religious quarrels, especially after the influences of Calvinism began to reach the country, mainly in the sphere of the Czech Unity of Brethren, which at times fell out with Lutheranism. It was at least a partial success that representatives of the Unity of Brethren, and of the official Utraquist Church agreed in 1575 upon a common faith, the so-called Bohemian Confession, which Maximilian promised to keep. Still more serious was the social disunity, as the interests of the high nobility opposed the interests of the lower nobility and the towns, not to mention the subjected peasants. This was the situation, when in 1576 Maximilian suddenly died and his son Rudolph II succeeded to the throne. In the great spiritual alignment, which, from the time of the Council of Trento and of the foundation of the Jesuit Order gradually divided Europe into two camps – Protestant North and Catholic South – Rudolph became an adherent of the second camp. He had spent the greater part of his young days in Spain, where he contracted a hatred for non-Catholics and antipathy for constitutional government. Although he made Prague the capital of his Empire, his relation to the Czech nation remained cold. He was no statesman himself – he was more interested in the arts and had a lively enthusiasm for the sciences – and also he was not a healthy man – and therefore he left the cares of government to a small number of persons whom he trusted. It is unnecessary to say that this court-clique, which gradually occupied all important official positions in the country, consisted of representatives of the Catholic, the "Spanish" party. As the number of Catholics in Bohemia did not exceed one-tenth or one-seventh at most, the exclusiveness of the Catholics meant the depriving of the majority of the nation of all political influence and was bound to create resistance.

Under these circumstances the time of Rudolph brought little good to the Czech nation. Rudolph's interest in arts and his collecting acti-

Jan Hus and Martin Luther
Administer the Holy Communion in Both Kinds
A wood-carving, Cranachian School,
1st half of 15th c.

vity for a time enriched the Castle of Prague, but had no influence upon the progress of popular art in the country. Neither did Rudolph's interest in astrology and alchemy meet with a response outside university circles. Although Czech literature made unexpected progress during Rudolph's reign, it had, on the whole, nothing in common with the milieu of the court in Prague. Its chief contribution, the Bible of Kralice, was the work of Moravian members of the Unity of Brethren; many of the significant works of this time did not find favour with the censorship, which was entrusted to the Catholic Archbishop, and remained in manuscript form. The Rudolphine literature belonged, in its nature, to the popular humanism, which paved the .way for the flowering which had been hindered by political storms.

The international character of Rudolph's court, where besides the alchemists Edward Kelly and John Dee the Dane Tycho de Brahe and the German Kepler were at work along with Czech and other courtiers, accentuated only more rapidly the spiritual lines of division among the Czech nobility. In an epoch in itself materialistic, the internationalism of Rudolph's reign had only bad effects. The nobles, who after the fall of the free towns were the sole political representatives of the medieval Czech nation, cultivated "pride of nobility" more than anything else, changed religion as it profited and placed their own privileges above the general good.

In the double quarrel of sovereign with nobility, the quarrel for religion and ways of government, a conflict broke out during Rudolph's reign in other Hapsburg countries as well as in Bohemia. In 1605 an anti-Hapsburg revolution broke out in Hungary, in 1608 in Austria. The Austrian Estates were joined by the Moravian Estates, in whose country Rudolph also entrusted the Catholic minority with the rule, all the worse as the Catholics were mostly foreigners. The 1608 revolution was not anti-dynastic in itself, it was led by Rudolph's brother Matthias. Rudolph retained the Bohemian throne only at the price of issuing an Imperial Charter, i. e. Letter of Majesty, a list of religious rights proclaimed in 1609 and signed also by Matthias. This Imperial Charter recognised the older Bohemian Confession and guaranteed religious freedom in a way corresponding to the Czech tradition of tolerance and by its care for the religious freedom of the peasants anticipated laws of toleration in the rest of Europe by a whole century. In 1611 Rudolph

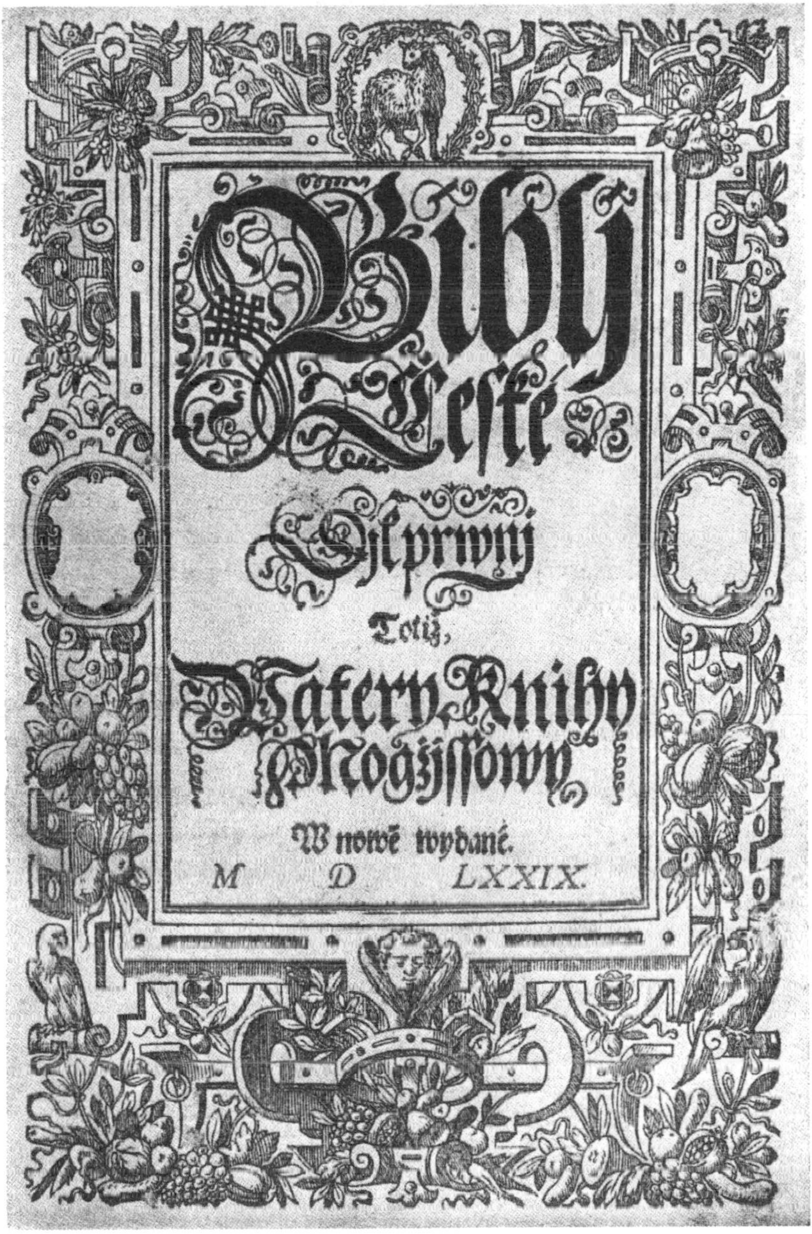
Biblj České
Djl prwnj
Totiž,
Patery Knihy Mogžiſſowy
W nowě wydané.
M D LXXIX.

The Title-page of the Bible published by the Unity of Brethren

tried to stem this progress, but in vain. He was dethroned and in the next year he died insane.

When in 1612 Matthias succeeded to the Bohemian throne, the Czech Protestants were to a great extent disillusioned. The candidate of the revolting Protestants changed into a sovereign who in the tradition of the Hapsburgs stood decisively on the anti-Reformation side. Anti-Hapsburg sentiment, strengthened by the excentricities of Rudolph's court and by the open support of the aggressive Catholics, came into existence once more. As the Czech schools suffered from the interference of religious opponents, Czech students went abroad, returning either as unyielding adherents to the ideas of the Reformation in the fashion of Wittenberg, Heidelberg or Geneva, or as fanatical followers of Rome or Spain. And so a line was drawn up and down the Czech countries and within each class of Czech society, dividing two different religions and two different political camps.

The diplomacy of the Catholic camp was more skillful: in 1617, a great success was scored, when the political adroitness of the Catholic party elected as Matthias's successor Ferdinand II, who until then had reigned in Styria, and who was known for his cruel persecution of his non-Catholic subjects. Emboldened by this success, the Catholic governors in Bohemia made several blunders, by which they manifestly violated the provisions of the Imperial Charter. The Protestant Bohemian nobility, afraid of losing their privileges, no less than of losing their religious liberty, summoned a meeting in Prague in spring of 1618 and on May 23rd threw two governors out of the windows of the Prague Castle. So began the Bohemian War, which was a prelude to the long European tragedy of the Thirty Years' War.

The Ludvík Wing in Prague Castle
Out of its windows two governors were thrown in 1618

VIII

THE FALL OF THE KINGDOM OF BOHEMIA

In 1618 nobody, certainly, suspected that the revolution in Bohemia would give an impetus to a fire which would in time inflame almost all Europe. That this was so is to be attributed equally to the radicals of both parties who in the Czech affair saw an occasion for the rousing of a final struggle between Catholicism and the Reformation, between the idea of the Spanish Empire and Absolutism and the idea of the liberty of the Estates and provincial self-administration. There is no doubt that the majority of Czechs were in favour of the anti-Hapsburg revolt. Apart from religious sympathies and antagonisms, cultural affinities played a great part. This appeared clearly in 1619 when after the death of Matthias, the young Frederick, the Elector Palatinate, the husband of Elizabeth, daughter of the English King James the First and sovereign of a small Rhineland province fertilised by French influences was elected King. The followers of Frederick of the Palatinate were members of the Unity of Brethren, many of whose leaders had studied at Heidelberg or Geneva, or even in England or the Scottish St. Andrews. The Czechs therefore, in the European struggle between North and South, chose for king a prince from the West, through whom they expected to gain the support of German Protestants, of Holland, England and perhaps also of France as allies, not forgetting in the meantime to win the Moravian, Silesian, Austrian and Hungarian Estates. A professor of the University of Prague, a Slovak by birth, John Jesenius, was sent to Transylvania in order to win the duke Gabriel Bethlen as ally.

The political plans of the Bohemian Estates did not lack ambition, but they were hardly realised. Dynastic reasons made the English king,

Queen Elizabeth of Bohemia
A copper-plate by an anonymous artist

James I, accept a careful policy of negotiations and neutrality; religious interests forced the French king, Louis XIII, to take measures in favour of the Catholic party. By the conclusion of the Treaty of Ulm in spring of 1620, the German Protestants abandoned their Czech co-religionists and their king, and the Elector of Saxony went over openly to the Emperor's side on promise of the Slavonic Lusatia. The Czechs and their Central European allies were not together sufficient to oppose the united forces of Catholic Europe. On November 8, 1620, they were defeated in battle on the White Mountain outside Prague, "championing a good cause ineffectively, while their adversaries brought an unworthy cause to victory", as the English Minister Plenipotentiary in Vienna, Henry Wotton, wrote.

The White Mountain meant a tragic end for the revolution and the beginning of the Calvary of the Czech nation; it did not, however, bring peace to Europe, as the Western European peace-makers supposed. The situation was better appreciated by the Czech pedagogue, Komenský (Comenius), who complained that "Bohemia bore the first burden of the attack" and its destruction gave the others time to prepare themselves for the inevitable struggle. While this struggle was tearing all Europe for thirty years, the Czech countries were passing through a painful regeneration, the like of which is seldom to be seen in history. The new Emperor, Ferdinand II, took the old Jesuit advice, "to destroy Luther's servants by sword, fire, water and rope", very literally. His vengeance reached not only the leaders of the revolt, who were executed in 1621 on the monumental Old Town Square of Prague. Because he needed money to pay an army of adventurers from all Europe, he confiscated the property of all who had stood against him in the revolution. As these made up nearly all the wealthy inhabitants of the kingdom, the expropriation of all national property took place in Bohemia and Moravia in the years following the White Mountain. Since the Catholic sovereign would not endûre heretics in his country, as much as a fourth of the free inhabitants emigrated for the sake of creed. Very few returned from emigration, and as the best people were included in it, the loss was irreparable for the nation as a whole. As the Thirty Years' War, especially in its later stages, brought ruin to the Czech countries, destroyed the towns, villages and commerce, depopulated Czech territory, the Czech nation lost, by the end of the war, two whole social classes, the nobility and the bourge-

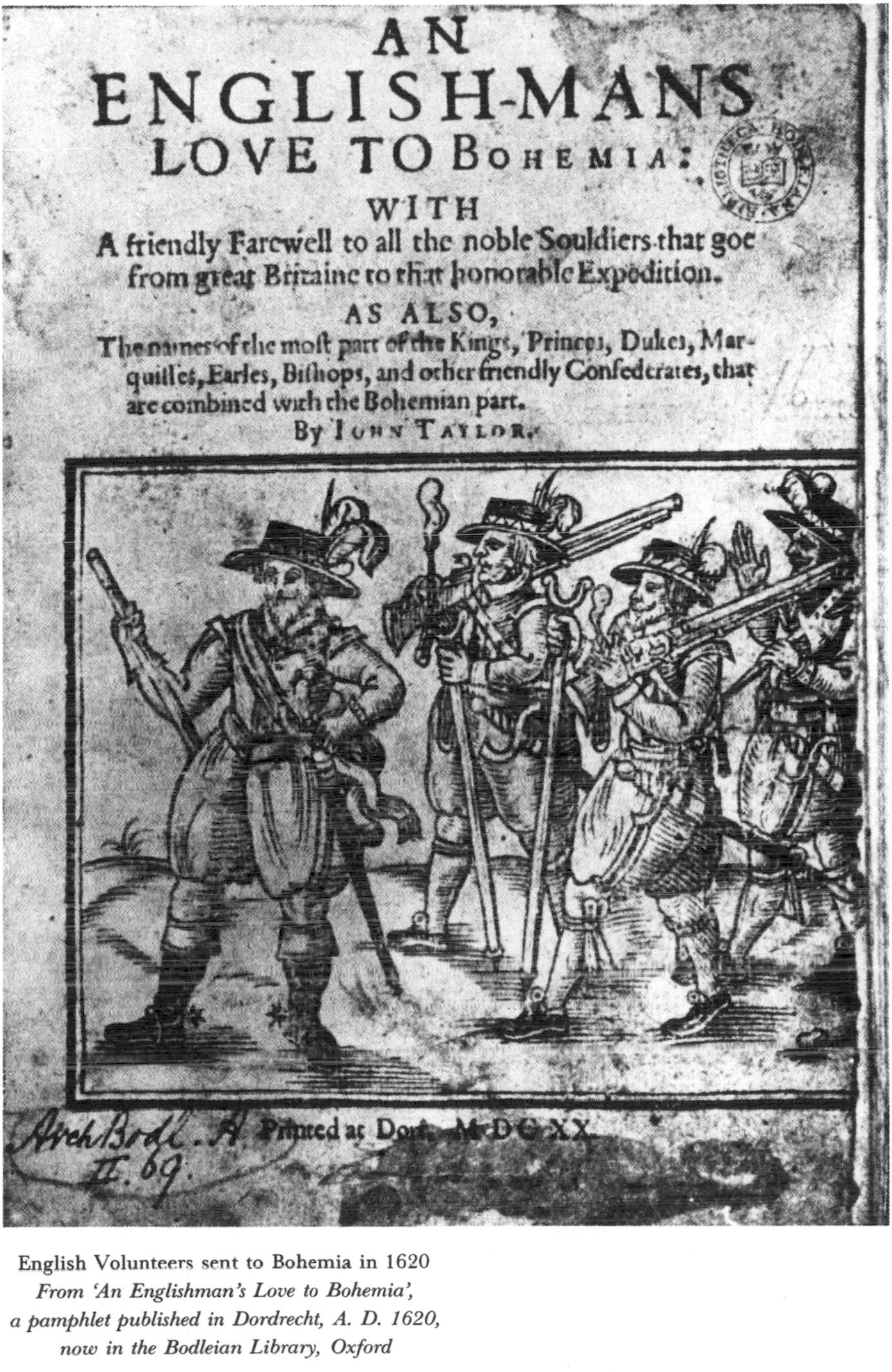
AN
ENGLISH-MANS
LOVE TO BOHEMIA:
WITH
A friendly Farewell to all the noble Souldiers that goe from great Britaine to that honorable Expedition.
AS ALSO,
The names of the most part of the Kings, Princes, Dukes, Marquisses, Earles, Bishops, and other friendly Confederates, that are combined with the Bohemian part.
By IOHN TAYLOR.

Printed at Dort. M.DC.XX.

English Volunteers sent to Bohemia in 1620
From 'An Englishman's Love to Bohemia',
a pamphlet published in Dordrecht, A. D. 1620,
now in the Bodleian Library, Oxford

oisies, which means nearly all the intelligentsia, the greatest part of the national property, the old faith with its cultural traditions and was, slowly but surely, losing even its own language. Adventurers from all the countries of Europe were coming in to occupy the places of the driven-out Czech ruling classes – a "foreign nation" of nobles and guards of the "rebel nation", which was already only a nation of peasants and city proletariat.

These masses of people, this "misera plebs contribuens", the true basis of the nation, remained, however, unbroken in the moral and national sense. While the renegades within the class of the nobility were rapidly losing contact with the nation and coming under the influence of the international milieu of the imperial court in Vienna and the rest of the patriciate were merging with the new German citizens in the towns, the people remained unbroken by misery and terror. At that time the character of the Czech nation as it is today was being formed. A united whole, popular and democratic in expression, anti-dynastic and rebellious in spirit. What a difference between the treachery of Albert of Wallenstein, a renegade from the Czech Unity of Brethren, who helped to destroy his country-men, built for the Hapsburgs their first standing army, reached for the Bohemian crown and in the end died at the hand of assassins at Cheb (Eger) in 1634 and the hard defence of East Moravian peasants and shepherds from Wallachia, who remained true to the old faith and to their leaders in exile for two generations, who allied with enemies of the Hapsburg Emperor and were defeated only in spring 1645 after the departure of the Swedish troops! Thousands of dead, lands burnt out, inhabitants moved by force – all this was familiar to the Czech countries even in the 17th century, at the hands of that same nation of lords and tyrants, who recently returned to the old methods of murder and rule.

But the difference between the behaviour of the typical aristocrat and the common person is also explained by the cold attitude of the Czech nation as a whole toward the imperious ambition of Wallenstein. The Czech State was broken by the constitution of the year 1627 from which all traces of the old religion and the national toleration were carefully removed. German soon became the first language of the country. The Slavonic element suffered an irreparable loss in the tearing away of Lusatian Serbia in 1635; it went to the Elector of Saxony for having betrayed his Czech co-religionists for the second

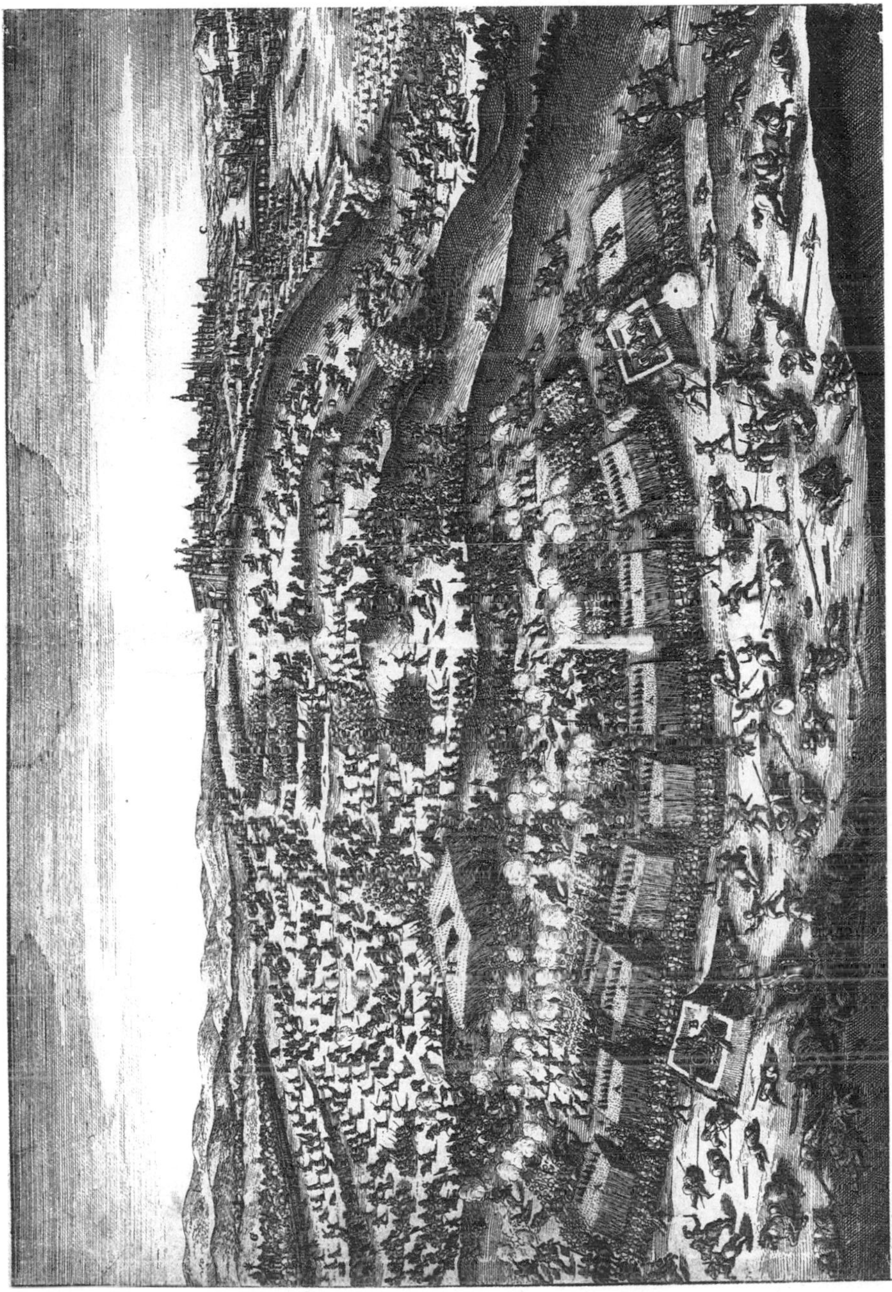

The Battle on the White Mountain
A copper-plate by Matouš Merian

time. In Lusatian Serbia the Czech State lost a territory, which had been part of it for three centuries without interruption. Moreover, the Czech State was governed from Vienna, and was only not eliminated because the Hapsburg sovereigns now and then needed its existence. When the Thirty Years' War was brought to an end by a peace-treaty at the Westphalian towns of Münster and Osnabrück, several of the principles for which the Czechs had been fighting long before were won in the negotiations. Religion was separated from politics for good, the existence of Protestantism was guaranteed, and the principle of peace-negotiations established. The Czech countries, however, remained in the possession of the Hapsburg Ferdinand III, and the hopes of those who had emigrated in the possibility of help from foreign allies were bitterly disappointed. Comenius, then a persecuted wandering Bishop of the Unity of Brethren, was writing his "Testament of the dying Mother, the Unity of Brethren" in the bitter knowledge that the Czechs had been sacrificed. He rejected tempting offers from England where, in accordance with his pansophistic ideas, the Royal Society was being founded as well as offers from America to combine activity at Harvard with work among the Indians, because he did not want to be too far away from his own country. Although his educational ideals, like his practical school-apparatus, were not allowed in Bohemia, this great man of the Czech nation, called by Michelet the "Galileo of Education", hoped for a better future for the sorely tried nation. And his compatriots in Poland and Slovakia, who through their work and their lives were building a bridge between the Czech countries and their new homes, shared his belief. The great duty of caring for the preservation of the tradition of Czechoslovak culture rested for one and a half centuries on what is today Slovakia. This duty Slovakia fulfilled, in spite of the lasting danger of Turkish invasions, in spite of civil wars and a growing oppression on the part of Hungarian magnates and the Catholic hierarchy. The spirit of revolt against overwhelming forces was shown even in Slovakia. The Slovak hero Jánošik, a strange robber, who took from the rich to gave to the poor, is typical of the same popular feeling as his fellows showed – Ondráš and Juráš in Moravia, and last but not least John Kozina Sladký, a courageous defender of the privileges of free men in the Western Bohemian district of the Chods. The sentiments of the people were not affected by the fact that their heroes met death on

A Portrait of Albert of Wallenstein
Oil on canvass, early 17th c.

the scaffold. They were heroes, because they represented the resistance-spirit of the nation, that was unable to fight as a whole.

The treaty of Westphalia brought the final breach between the emigrés and the people at home. Such noble figures as the Czech historian Pavel Skála, the engraver W. Hollar toiling in London, Comenius writing in Polish Leszno and the Dutch Amsterdam and J. Holík in the Baltic lands together only hint at the possibilities withdrawn from the nation in its own country. Of course the culture of Old Bohemia did not perish at one stroke. Another generation of Baroque and Catholic poets was bred on the old cultural heritage. At the very end of the 17th century Czech Catholicism gave the language a passionate defender in the historian Bohuslav Balbín, a member of the militant Jesuit Order. Of course, Balbín's ecclesiastical superiors looked on his activities with suspicion and consequently most of his writings remained for another century concealed in manuscript.

Popular chronicles, compiled by dilettante historians in towns and villages contain at the end of the 17th century a collection of sneers and nicknames the object of which was invariably the Hapsburg Emperor Leopold I. Leopold was unpopular among the Czechs, although his chief adviser was for two decades a nobleman from Bohemia, W. Eusebius of Lobkowicz. Great families of the Czech nobility prospered and gave the country more than one building of artistic value – but they had already little in common with the people: the age of Leopold brought to Bohemia the development of Baroque architecture and prepared for the growth of the Czech baroque music, but it did not in the least help Czech literature. The explanation is simple: the speech of arts and music is not so dangerous to the régime, because it does not express the genius of the nation directly. The writer creates his work in private, and his manuscript can survive decades to become eloquent in the better future. A symphony and a church building are nothing before they have been realized by material means. Therefore the Czech Baroque is poor in literature and rich in arts and music.

The already exhausted country had to bear further exertions for the Emperor's wars. The Turkish invasions of 1663 and 1683 devastated Moravia and Slovakia, as Hungary, the "decus Europae" of the Magyar historians, was at this time only too willing to help the Turks. The besieged Vienna was defended by J. Kaplíř of Sulevic, the offspring of

IOHAN·AMOS COMENIVS, MORAVVS. A° ÆTAT 50. 164
Exsump. M. S:
G. Glouer. fe:
Loe, here an Exile: who to serue his God
Hath sharply tasted of proud Pashurs Rod
Whose learning, Piety, & true worth, being knowne
To all the world, makes all the world his owne
F: Q

Comenius
Clover's drawing

a family of rebels – and it was relieved by King John Sobieski of Poland. From that time the Turkish danger ceased. Southern Hungary was re-settled by Serbian and Slovak colonists and at least in part the contact between Southern and Western Slavs was resumed.

The Battle of the White Mountain, which struck the name of Bohemia off the list of independent European States, indirectly wrought upon the consciousness of the Slavonic nations. This Slavonic consciousness can be found in the Catholic Balbín as much as in the Protestant Comenius. In his "History of the Persecution of the Bohemian Church" Comenius and his collaborators even tried to revive the idea of Great Moravia. The connections with Poland and Slovakia, the renewed links with the Southern Slavs, the pride caused by the heroism of King John Sobieski, and the vague knowledge of the ambitious personage of the Russian Czar Peter the Great were able to survive this age.

The successors of Leopold kept on asking new victims from Bohemia. During the wars against the Turks and especially during the struggle with France, the imperialism of Louis XIV united the whole Continent against France and caused a coalition whose generals were Marlborough and Prince Eugene of Savoy and among whose creators was another Bohemian diplomatist – Count Wratislaw of Mitrovice. The Czech lands continued to furnish the basic taxation and the bulk of the troops. When the last Hapsburg, Charles VI (1711–1740), tried to secure the throne to his eldest daughter Maria Theresa, the idea of the independent Crown of Bohemia was temporarily revived. At the same time a new wave of religious persecution swept over the country, for Charles wished to gain the support of the Catholic hierarchy. Again fires blazed at the stakes – instead of heretics the Czech heretic books were being burnt. The Jesuit Koniáš was especially proud of the fact that he burnt 60,000 books all by himself. Obstinate heretics were objects of dragonades, they were being sent to galleys, sometimes they toiled to death in the salt mines of Transylvania or in Hungarian fortresses. Those who did not want to succumb found their way high up into the mountains or over the frontiers. Eastern Moravia, where one century before Comenius had been active as a minister, was the home of a group of descendants of the members of the Unity of Brethren. They found refuge in Lusatia and a protector in Count Zinzendorf. The Lusatian Herrenhut became the printing centre

Fighting the Turks
An oil-painting by Václav Vavřinec Rainer

where Czech clandestine books were published. There too were trained those ardent missionaries, usually called the "Moravian Brethren". Their example was felt in England, where they founded schools at Fulneck near Leeds, at Fairfield, near Manchester, near Derby, and an active community in London. They did not fail to influence the Protestant revival in the Methodism of John Wesley.

Even at home the old religions was not completely forgotten. In 1729 John of Pomuk, called Nepomucenus, was proclaimed Saint, in order to bury in oblivion the memory of another John, Master John Hus. A legend told about him that he died martyr's death under Wenceslas IV, trying to preserve the secret of the Confession. His memory, and the cult of other Czech saints as well, was carried far by the Czech members of the Jesuit order. These Jesuits organized dramatic performances in Moscow, compiled grammars in the tongues of Asiatic tribes, and settled as monks in South America. In Bohemia, the new Saint found his place on the bridges. Finally he became quite popular among the Czech rebels, who said of him that he was their patron – like him, they too had to be silent in their own country, ruled by aliens.

The Chapel and School Fulneck near Leeds

A contemporary English print

IX

THE AGE OF ENLIGHTENED ABSOLUTISM

The last years of Charles VI's reign witnessed in the Czech lands the re-emergence of new currents of Western European thought. Among them were the French Jansenism and the Anglo-French philosophy of Enlightenment. When Charles' daughter Maria Theresa (1740–80) ascended the throne, the retreat of the Italian court culture was complete and the influence of French literature and philosophy prevalent. The representative of this French type of culture was of course much more the rival of Maria Theresa, King Frederick II of Prussia, than the Queen of Bohemia and Hungary, as was her official title.

It was partly due to the influence of the Western European philosophy of state that the Prussian state was considerably better equipped for the Frederician era of German imperialism. The position of the Hapsburg Queen was the more constrained as her dominions became more exhausted. They were soon attacked by a hungry coalition, headed by France. In the ensuing struggle Bohemia was again a continental battlefield, assuming her old role of Central European bulwark.

In November 1741 this bulwark was captured by a Franco-Bavarian army, and Charles Albert, ruler of Bavaria, was on the 7th of December elected King of Bohemia. The fates were not favourable to this Wittelsbach Prince, whose ancestor was Maximilian of Bavaria who triumphed over the Bohemians in 1620 in the Battle of the White Mountain. Charles Albert, although he was elected Emperor of the Holy Roman Empire, did not reign longer than once did the Winter King. In 1742 the French retreated from Prague, and that was the end of the last revolt of the Bohemian feudality. This time no reign of terror followed. Maria Theresa's position was not strong enough to challenge the nobility. The fate of several villages, whose inhabitants believed in Charles Albert's promises of abolishing serfdom and giving freedom from taxation and who fought against the Hapsburg army, was not much better than the fate of modern Lidice. The Czechs again became suspicious, they revived the old tradition of rebellion, and all this probably helped to overcome scruples when the rest of Czech state institutions were being abolished.

The battle of Bohemia brought the maximum of profit to Frederick II. He got by the Treaty of Berlin (1742) the whole of Silesia, with the exception of the old principalities of Opava, Těšín and Krnov. The so-called second war of Silesia, frustrated by a treaty in 1745 only confirmed the Prussian serfdom of Silesia. After Lusatia, lost in 1635, when the treacherous Elector of Saxony got it as a reward, Silesia was the second loss for the old unit of the Bohemian crown. Western Silesia was then a prey to Germanization, backed by the old Protestant sympathies. The ruler of Prussia assumed the role of Protector of Protestant subjects of the Hapsburgs, of course only in so far as it was profitable for his policy.

The following short period of rest was used by Maria Theresa for a reorganisation of her dominions. The altruistic source and inspiration for her reforms was without doubt the French rationalism. The so-called enlightened absolutism, since the time of Maria Theresa the semi-official state philosophy, tried to realize reforms from above. The result for Bohemia was the destruction of the last remnants of the old self-government of the Estates. Especially the year 1748 became important for the history of the Czech administration. In that year, the Estates of Bohemia consented to raise taxes for a whole decade and thus lost their last weapon. The old Court Chancellery of Bohemia was abolished as the last office, up to that time representing the once-independent Kingdom of Bohemia. The old lands of the Crown were thenceforward governed by a new office, common for Bohemia and Austria. Hungary retained her old special position – because there the government of the Estates was still alive.

The preparations for the final duel between Prussia and the Habsburg dominions, usually called Austria, were completed by the Chancellor Wenceslas of Kaunitz. He was descended from an old Moravian noble family, long ago absorbed by the Viennese court. He succeeded in the famous "renversement des alliances" – the radical change in the grouping of European powers. England, for decades an ally of Austria, became allied to Prussia, and France became united with the Habsburgs. This change influenced the cultural development of the country, because it was impossible to oppose the French influence openly.

The Seven Years' War between Prussia and Austria, and between England and France gradually became the first world-war. All the European powers became involved in the struggle, including Russia, and the fate of the colonial empires was being resolved on the Bohemian battlefields. At the very beginning of the fighting the Prussians came as far as Prague, and caused considerable damage by bombing the besieged city. They did not succeed and they were defeated at the battle of Kolín in 1757. Prussian militarism was crushed by victorious Russian troops invading Berlin. England succeeded in destroying the colonial power of France. Nevertheless, the political structure of Central Europe remained unchanged by the Treaty of 1763. The Czech lands remained a bulwark against Hohenzollern expansion to the South. They were of course ravaged by the war, and the situation of the peasants and working classes in the towns was desperate. These classes bore the whole brunt of taxation on their shoulders, and Bohemia alone yielded 32–49% of the taxes of the whole monarchy! Hunger and peasants' risings were therefore continual consequences of the situation.

In 1765 Maria Theresa's son, the Emperor Joseph II, became co-regent. Young Goethe noticed Prince Joseph's irreverent behaviour during the coronation ceremonies at Frankfurt. Joseph II was the spiritual opposite of his mother in many ways. He did not like the Catholic Church and conservative political thought. He consented to his mother's imperialist expansion towards the East, where Galicia was gained by Maria Theresa during the first partition of Poland in 1772. "Elle pleurait mais elle prenait toujours," wrote the cynical Frederick II of the behaviour of his rival during the Polish crisis. Maria Theresa, who in 1748 destroyed the last remnants of the independent Kingdom of Bohemia, was among those who destroyed the Kingdom of Poland. By the end of the 18th century, Russia was the only Slavonic state, and her power was increasing.

The dissolution of the Jesuit Order (1773) was accepted with horror by Maria Theresa, while Joseph II did not try to hide his joy. Joseph tried to defend the Bohemian peasants, when they started a hopeless hunger-revolt in 1775. In 1777, the flames of discontent and rebellion appeared in Moravian Wallachia, where Protestant traditions were kept alive by ministers coming from Silesia and Slovakia. This time persecution was prevented by Joseph, who threatened his mother with abdication, should religious persecution take place in his future empire. The rebellion in Moravia has another significance too: it showed the disapproval of the brutal Counter-Reformation methods by the clergy of the 18th century. Under the influence of the liberal philosophy of Jansen and Pascal, the clergy advocated religious tolerance and a friendly attitude to the people.

On account of his attitude towards the popular classes, Joseph's reign (1780–90) was awaited with great hopes, especially by the peasants. Many of these hopes remained unfulfilled. First of all Joseph did not believe in tolerance, his intolerance merely put enlightenment of the Prussian type on the pedestal of the Catholic Church. Josephinism is therefore the cumulative name of the concentrated idea of absolute state. The old means of brutal power were realizing by will of the ruler some of the principles of Western European enlightenment. Incongruence of ideas and means of realization were the cause of the final wreck of Joseph's work.

Joseph was no revolutionary, and even the most radical of his reforms, the abolition of serfdom (1781) meant no revolutionary changes in the country. Its importance lies in the fact that it made possible the emancipation of the peasants, and a better education for their sons. The edict of religious tolerance, issued the same year, gave religious freedom to the followers of Lutheran, Calvinist and Orthodox religions. 45,000 Protestants were not allowed to return to the old ideals of the Unity of Brethren. Nevertheless, new contacts were made possible between Czech and Slovak Protestants, and many ministers of Slovak and Magyar origin came over from Hungary and helped to establish the Czech Protestant church. In 1784 many monasteries and churches were closed by the Emperor's order. Occasionally, buildings of artistic value and cultural treasures of old convents were destroyed. But many old Czech books were re-discovered for contemporary readers and became accessible once more, after nearly two centuries of monastic seclusion.

Thus Joseph's reforms, seen from the Czech standpoint, had both favourable and unfavourable results. Joseph did not realize the strength of national ideas, did not believe in tradition and historical development. In his view, the German language was especially suitable to become the lingua franca of Central Europe. It is remarkable, however, that he arranged for the publication in Czech of all important decrees, that he did not prevent the publishing of Czech books and apologies for the Czech language, and that the Royal Bohemian Society of Sciences was founded during his reign (1784), the first scientific society in Bohemia.

Advantages given by Joseph to the German language were defended on practical grounds, and were copied by later Austrian politicians. Joseph failed to notice that his monarchy became a state of nationalities, especially after the failure to exchange the Austrian Netherlands for Bavaria. The Hapsburg monarchy gained new Slavonic subjects in the Eastern Carpathians, and a war with Turkey and the alliance with Russia was to add new Slavonic territories to Joseph's state. Temporary military failures, revolts in Belgium and Hungary and consumption prematurely broke the Emperor who witnessed from his deathbed the end of most of his reforms.

In the history of Central Europe Joseph II remains an example of a ruler, who could not find the means appropriate for realizing his ideas. The Czechs did not agree in their views on Joseph; some of them protested against the Emperor's reforms, and defended old ways and privileges. Others were grateful to him for his liberation of the peasants and idealized his personage. Generally speaking, the conservative classes, the clergy and the nobility (led by the members of the families of Taaffe and MacNeven) and exceptional individuals from the peasantry (such as the chronicler F. J. Vavák) were strongly against Joseph and his work. All those who were in touch with European thought showed a positive attitude to Joseph. These classes represented a minority of the clergy, a handful of intellectuals and a few nobles, like the historian and soldier Jan Jeník of Bratřice.

By his reforms Joseph awakened in the Czech lands forces which aimed at goals different from those of Josephinism. The protection of German culture brought a certain number of renegades to the Germans, but it gave impulse to passionate apologies for the Czech language. The final end of the old idea of a state, governed by the Estates, gave way to the territorial patriotism of the nobility. Very

Initiation Ceremonies in a Freemasons' Lodge
An oil-painting by Ignác Unterberger (?)

often this patriotism apparently concealed material reasons for opposition to the Emperor, who was the first to submit state property to taxation. The nobility opened its archives to Czech historians, hoping they would find there arguments for the struggle with the Emperor. Thus the struggle of the nobility coincided with the revival of historical study in the Czech nation. The "local" patriotism of the nobility had (usually) little to do with the evolution of the Czech intelligentsia. The backbone of this was the clergy who followed the example of Balbín in uniting Catholicism with the Czech cultural feeling. In the 18th century the church was nearly the only place from which the Czech language was not banned. The popularized Catholicism (the representative of which is the chronicler Vavák) made possible the saying of K. Čapek: "Since the time of the national revival, Czech Protestantism is not anti-Catholic and there is a trace of Hussite feeling in every Czech Catholic."

The reaction of the clergy against Joseph's interference in Church matters led them to a realisation of the importance of the national consciousness. Not only in Bohemia, in Slovakia too was revived "historia Bohemica" at the Catholic University of Trnava. At the same time Czech and Slovak Protestants looked proudly back at the old tradition of the non-Catholic culture, whose fruits were slowly being made accessible to readers. A guardian of old traditions was in the same way Matej Bél, rector of Bratislava, or Jan Jeník of Bratřice, a Catholic whose tolerance did not shrink before accusations of Catholics and Protestants alike. Jeník, who was first fascinated by the philosophy of Enlightement, later became interested in old documents, and that study helped him to realize the value of the Hussite and Protestant Czech culture from the times before the White Mountain.

All these intellectuals, few in number and followers of various spiritual movements, have nevertheless two things in common. First of all, they all believed in the future of the Slavonic nations. This racial consciousness was influenced in the next generation by Romanticism and the philosophy of Hegel. Secondly, they highly esteemed the Czech peasant as representative of the Czech revolting classes. The peasants were for the first modern Czech patriots the guarantee of the national existence, they were the future leading class of the nation.

From this point of view the five decades of the reign of Maria Theresa and Joseph II are a preparatory period. Future development was being prepared: the remnants of feudalism were broken and gave way to a reorganization of the economic background against which the world of Baroque was being transformed into the world of Liberalism. The Czech peasantry supplied the factories of the early 19th century with workers, and peasants, workers and intellectuals have since that time formed the components of the structure of the nation.

X

THE RENAISSANCE OF THE CZECH PEOPLE

Leopold II (1790–1792), brother and successor of Joseph II, is taken by some historians, to be the best Hapsburg monarch. The judgement is rather obscured by the fact that the reign of this enlightened monarch from Italian Tuscany did not last long. His first task was to restore order in his restless empire. The peace treaty wirth Turkey stopped expansion into the Balkans. He tactfully pacified Belgium; against the restless Hungarian Estates he used the help of the South Hungarian Serbs; Czech goodwill was won by his coronation as King of Bohemia on Sep. 6th 1791. Mozart composed an opera especially for this occasion and a young Czech scholar, Joseph Dobrovský, made a speech in which he emphasized the importance of the loyalty of Czechs and Slavs generally for the existence of the Hapsburg Empire. Although Leopold did not go back on the principles existing before 1748, he nevertheless granted valuable concessions to Czech national feeling, which was dominated for the time by its conservative elements. A Chair of Czech Language was inaugurated at the University of Prague, which meant a great deal to a modest nation deprived for two centuries of all basic cultural institutions.

Leopold's untimely death after two years of rule meant a partial liquidation of Joseph's reforms. That does not imply that all the good work of Joseph and its fruits were nullified. There were numerous scholars and men of education even among the clergy and the bureaucracy, and they remained faithful to the ideas of enlightenment. In spite of the absolutism of the police state and the strict censorship, introduced by Leopold's nephew Francis II (1782–1835), some of the privileges of the previous period survived. Francis II, a conservative

A Portrait of Josef Dobrovský
An oil-painting by František Tkadlík

and incompetent ruler, made an end to all progress in Austria, as he lived continually under the dread of the French Revolution against which his predecessor had started to fight. Wars against France did not bring many laurels to the Austrian armies. One campaign after another was lost and brought heavy losses in men – recruited mostly from the Slavonic parts of the Empire.

The French Revolution and Napoleon's reign were greeted with enthusiasm in Poland; in Hungary secret groups supported France and the police régime was kept busy suppressing them. In Bohemia there was no such response; the people were only starting to awake, and there were not enough enlightened men who would have understood happenings of European importance. This does not mean that there were none. The aforementioned historian, John Jeník of Bratřice, who took part in the first campaigns against France, gives an interesting picture in his memoirs of the feelings of a Czech intellectual grown up in the period of Enlightenment and therefore full of admiration for the ideals of the French Revolution and the bravery of the French armies against whom in the end he refused to fight. But he was strictly opposed to Napoleon's imperialism; he refused to regard him as a great general and compared him unfavourably with the Republican general, Moreau. Returning from the wars, Jeník brought with him a national and a Slav consciousness which found expression in his interest not only in the Southern Slavs and Poles who lived under the same monarchy but in the Russians as well. The Russians fought in Suvarov's Army and were given a very warm welcome by Czech patriots who derived strength from the might of the Russian Army in their everyday fight for at least a weak flame of national existence.

The Slav consciousness was shared by Josef Dobrovský; through his studies of the old Slavonic language and through his trips to Russia, Dobrovský became the creator of the first programme of our Slavonic studies. With democratic feeling social consciousness revived. The French Wars gave an impetus to the beginning of industry in the Czech lands, in many cases to industries so far unknown in Europe, as was the case with the sugar industry. Other branches of industry started as home-industries, as for instance the glass and clothiery. Unfortunately these industries were localized in the border regions only, where the inhabitans were German, so that the industralisation of Bohemia was a heavy blow to the Czech national entity. The social consciousness of those times can be found even in Czech literature. An apotheosis of the people is evident in a scene from a drama, where a general (the popular Charles of Schwarzenberg), member of a native noble family, distributes his medals among peasants and workers.

Such was the political background in the Czech lands in the eventful years when Napoleon was trying hard to dominate Europe. Bohemia, and even more Slovakia, were outside the main scenes of this fight. As far as Bohemia figured in Napoleon's plans, these remained unrealized because geography was strongly opposed to them. In 1805 an Austro-Russian army was defeated at Slavkov (Austerlitz) in Moravia and this moved Emperor Francis to the proclamation of the dissolution of the old Holy Roman Empire of the German nation. The Czechs remained indifferent to this decision. They were much more influenced by the Romantic belief in autonomous nations than by theories of historical right.

In 1809, Czech regiments stopped Napoleon at Wagram, and the French defeat of Leipzig (in 1813) once more showed the strategic importance of Bohemia. During the wars the Czech esteem of human beings found its expression in a generous care for the victims of the war. The Czechs welcomed the end of hostilities and the idealist endeavours of the Russian Czar Alexander, whose plan of the Holy Alliance had much in common with the ideas of King George of Poděbrady and Comenius. But the diplomacy of the Chancellor, Prince Metternich, transformed the Holy Alliance into a police institution whose primary task was the struggle against all possible revolutions. At home Metternich was much more enlightened. To preserve Austria he advocated the plan of a union of Czech and Polish lands into an administrative unit.

The first generation of Czech patriots, living under the threat of informers and haters of everything Slavonic, was able to do a good deal for the nation. The protection given by some of the noblemen was the heritage of the Josephine era. One of them, the scientist K. of Sternberg, became the founder of the Museum of the Kingdom of Bohemia in Prague. Sternberg and Dobrovský tried to revive the national consciousness and to give a new basis to a new national culture. Dobrovský, whose works became known in England at the end of the 18th century, died in 1829. The next year, 1830, was the year of revolutions. The secret societies of the "Young Europe" showed for

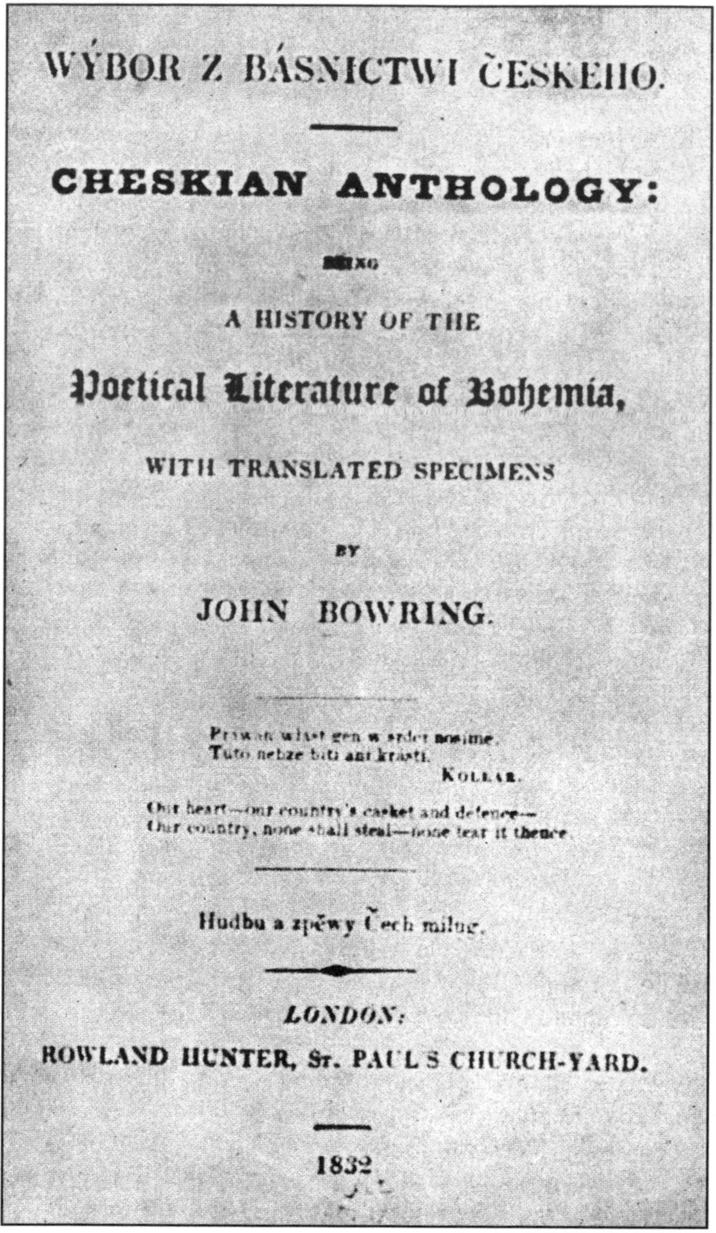

WÝBOR Z BÁSNICTWI ČESKEHO.

CHESKIAN ANTHOLOGY:

BEING

A HISTORY OF THE

Poetical Literature of Bohemia,

WITH TRANSLATED SPECIMENS

BY

JOHN BOWRING.

Prawau wlast gen w srdci nosime,
Tuto nelze biti ani krasti.

KOLLAR.

Our heart—our country's casket and defence—
Our country, none shall steal—none tear it thence.

Hudbu a zpěwy Čech miluge.

LONDON:

ROWLAND HUNTER, St. PAUL'S CHURCH-YARD.

1832

Cheskian Anthology by John Bowring

The title-page of the first survey of Czech literature

the first time their unexpected strength. The revolution in Poland found its supporters among young students in Bohemia and Moravia and gave impetus to a wave of interest in politics.

But the representatives of the second generation of pioneers, the heirs of Dobrovský, were no politicians – they were poets and scientists. The translator Josef Jungmann acquainted his countrymen with the best works of Western European literatures. He gave a model for younger translators in Milton's "Paradise Lost", but he was at the same time interested in a cultural Pan-Slavist movement and even preached the necessity of a common Slavonic literary language.

Many of the poets and thinkers of this period came from Slovakia, where old cultural traditions among Protestants and Catholics alike survived the 18th century. Thus, Slovakia was able to supply the representatives of the poetry of a Czechoslovak revival. Jan Kollár, a Slovak writing in Czech, believed in a union of Slavonic nations, of which Russia should be the head, Poland the body, Bohemia the arms and other nations, limbs. "What will be the fate of Europe and the Slavs in a century?" he asked. P. J. Šafařík, also a Slovak, living for years in Yugoslavian Novi Sad, was the author of "Slavonic Antiquities", highly appreciated especially in Russia, because this work was the first historical study of all Slavonic nations.

The representative of the third and last generation of the pioneers of a Czech revival, Francis Palacký, was a Protestant from Moravia, who spent his youth in Slovakia. Scottish and English historians were his teachers, and his philosophy of Romanticism was influenced by America and France. His view of Czech history had its foundation in the ideals of the Unity of Brethren and in his belief in Slavs, whose clash with Germans Palacky forecast.

The "History of the Czech Nation" by Palacký was published at the beginning of the reign of Emperor Ferdinand V (1835–48). Ferdinand was never quite normal and there were few changes during his reign. Metternich found a rival in Count Kolovrat, a Bohemian nobleman who was sympathetic to the Czech national movement. The conflict between the two leading men led to a complete stagnation of public life.

Thus criticism could appear once more, and the noblemen from Bohemia, now claiming their share in the government, did not spare the government. One of these nobles, Count Leo Thun, was the first to see the dangerous situation of the Slavs in Hungary. In 1843 he published his polemics with a Magyar journalist, Fr. Pulszky. Pulszky went so far as to threaten everyone writing in Czech with eviction from Hungary. This danger led the Slovak leaders, Ludevít Štúr and Jos. M. Hurban to the proclamation of the independent Slovak language (in 1844). Kollár, Šafařík and Palacký were against the secession. Political reasons gave rise to the independent Slovak nation, although the cultural losses, that had their source in isolation, were soon felt by a nation, still too feeble to lead an independent existence.

During the eighteen-forties the Czech nation was rapidly attaining its maturity. Political thought of Western Europe influenced the Czech political clubs the most renowned of which got the name of the "Repeal Club". The representative of the younger generation was the journalist, Karel Havlíček. In his work we find the nucleus of all the political problems of the 19th century. Under the influence of his personal experience, Havlíček put aside the uncritical belief in the Russian Czar. He drafted the programme of modern Czech democracy. He believed in the individuality of his nation but he understood the necessity for co-operation of the Czechs with other nations of Central Europe, especially with the Slavs.

This was approximately the programme proclaimed by the Czechs in 1848. In February of that year the Paris Revolution gave rise to a fire that finally spared only England and Russia. The Prague revolutionary movement preceded even that of Vienna, and the democratic members of the "Repeal Club" pushed into the background the aristocratic rebels. First of all, it was necessary to show the people the value of political freedom. Havlíček did his best to educate the people by his "National Newspaper".

The Pan-German movement whose followers assembled at Francfort divided the Czechs and the Germans whose relations had been quite friendly up to that time. Palacký had to refuse the invitation to Francfort because as a historian he knew that Bohemia had never had more in common with the German Reich than the feudal relation of ruler to Emperor. Bohemia was never a part of the Imperial administrative structure and German rulers had had no right to give laws to the Czechs. German liberals from Bohemia, now in a minority, did not fail to see in Palacký an arch-enemy.

Palacký was firmly convinced that the Hapsburg monarchy was for his Czech contemporaries the necessary condition of future national

A Portrait of František Palacký
An oil-painting by Josef Helich

growth. Later on, at the end of his life, after a series of disappointments, his opinion was different. Czech democratic politicians had now enemies in the Court and among the nobility. German liberals were unfriendly to their Czech neighbours, just as the Slovaks found no friends in Magyar revolutionary liberals under L. Kossuth.

This tragic conflict of political and national ideas was the cause of the early death of Austrian constitutionalism. In June, 1848, the Slavonic Congress was organized in Prague. Palacký was the leader of the Czechs, Vuk Karadžić of the Serbs, Bakunin was the representative of the Russian revolutionaries. On Whit Monday there was a clash between civilians and the army, commanded by the reactionary General Windischgraetz. Street fighting followed for five days, and that was the end of the Slavonic Congress. The rising was subdued and the military government made an end to the attempt to gain some sort of self-government for Bohemia. The Prague fire of revolution was extinguished. And when the Parliament was found too reluctant (it had a Slavonic majority), the revolution in Vienna and Hungary served as a pretext for its early suppression.

At least one reform resulted from this first period of Austrian constitutionalism: the old duties compelling peasants to work on their lords' fields were abolished. The peasants were now completety free and could take part in the struggle of nationalities. The parliament was transferred to Kroměříž in Moravia where it led a decrepit existence until spring of 1849. It survived the abdication of Emperor Ferdinand, who was followed by his youthful nephew, Francis Joseph I (1848–1916). The parliament prepared a draft of a progressive constitution, but had no time to implement it. The danger was over, revolution was defeated and thus it was possible to dissolve the Parliament. Even the "octroi" constitution never became effective. The breach between the conservative nobility from Bohemia and the Czech bourgeois leaders was complete.

The stormy year 1848 helped to inaugurate the cooperation of the Czech and other Slavonic nations of the Hapsburg monarchy. Czech volunteers helped the Slovaks against the Magyar revolution. The struggle in Hungary forced Emperor Francis Joseph to ask Czar Nicholas II for help. The Russian army crushed the revolt in Hungary, but the Slavonic allies of the Hapsburgs, the Croats, Serbs, Slovaks and Czechs waited in vain for a reward.

Thus the year 1848 did not realize all the promises offered to the organizers of the Slavonic Congress. Neither the Czechs nor the Slovaks achieved political gains. Racial hatred of their German and Hungarian neighbours reduced them to support the conservative dynasty, although their political ideals had little in common with it. Nevertheless, this year gave evidence of the vitality of the Czech nation. If it did not prove Czech political maturity, it was a sufficient testimony of Czech national vitality. And the experiences of 1848 became the basis of Czech policy in the next decades.

XI

THE STRUGGLE FOR POLITICAL DEMOCRACY

For ten years the Czechs and Slovaks were condemned to political passivity. The fates of Palacký and Havlíček were characteristic for the life of the Czech intelligentsia; the former was forced into the background by the threat of a court-martial, the latter sent, without trial, into exile in Tyrol, whence he returned home only to die. In this time of new absolutism Havlíček's funeral was an event of political importance and only the bravest marched behind the coffin of this ideal Czech journalist. On his coffin lay a wreath of thorns. The police terror pursuing a policy of centralisation and Germanization was supported by the Church of Rome whose representatives, at that time, made their interests identical with those of the dynasty. Only diplomatic setbacks which led to the isolation of Austria in Europe and the economic disaster of 1859 made an end to this sad interlude.

The reign of Francis Joseph I (1848–1916) is marked by this monarch's characteristic endeavour to evade responsibility and reforms. This led him to make promises to his Czech subjects whenever an internal crisis forced him to do so and to annul these when his position seemed stronger. The promise he made to the Czechs in 1860 was known as the October Diploma; it is superfluous to add that it was never kept. Nevertheless the constitutional course which the monarch started with the Diploma and followed for seven years makes this a critical period for the Hapsburg Monarchy. During this time Austria tried for the last time to fullfil her historical mission: to keep in check the growing pressure of Germany, coming from Berlin and pushing towards the East and South-East. The old Empire of Austria was especially ill-prepared for this task; the constitution was not effective

An Amazon on the Barricades
A scene from the Prague revolt in 1848,
from a contemporary print

and the domination of the feudal landowners, who were mostly Germans, was upheld only by a complicated voting arithmetic.

In spite of all, the Czech people flourished at this time. In 1862 the Sokol movement started. This organisation for physical culture was inspired by democratic and Slavonic ideals. In 1866, Smetana's opera "The Bartered Bride" revealed the Czech musical genius, as the paintings of Josef Mánes did in the arts. At this time too the Slovaks claimed their rights, sending a memorandum to the Emperor from Turč. Sv. Martin in 1861. But the seventy landowners in Parliament were hardly representative of the peoples within a monarchy whose Emperor broke his pledges and drove his Slavonic subjects into opposition. In his pamphlet "The Idea of the Austrian State", the ageing Palacký showed the danger of a German-Hungarian oppression and of dualism, considered by some politicians of the court-circle to be the latest cure for the disintegrating state.

In 1866 near the Bohemian town of Hradec Králové the Hapsburg Monarchy lost the war of "Germans against Germans" to Prussian military superiority. Bismarck showed far greater diplomatic leniency towards Austria than later to a conquered France. A division of the Czech lands was out of the question; only when he needed it did Bismarck promise to support the claims of Czech autonomy. The defeat meant the political end of old Austria, forced out of Italy and the German "Bund". The moment Austria became a satellite of Prussianized Germany, she lost her reason for existence. That this happened was the fault of the Hapsburg court which brought about the Austro-Hungarian "Ausgleich" (1867), legitimizing the division of the Monarchy into two parts dominated by Germans and Magyars respectively.

In the Austrian part the Germans were undoubtedly in a minority. In 1867 the landowning nobility was economically on the decline. They were willing to help the Germans to an artificial supremacy. Hence the final separation between the Czechs and Slovaks and their landowning gentry who became Germanized and Magyarized with astonishing speed. So Czech political leaders preferred to boycott a Parliament which was not representative of the population. By way of protest against foreign policy the Czech delegates paid a visit ostentatiously to the Moscow Exhibition (1867), and started discussions with the French Emperor Napoleon III. But they did so more in spontaneous protest than as an act of policy, for neither Russian Czar nor French Emperor showed particular interest in the Czechs, who were politically weak and adhered openly to democratic principles. And the Czech leaders remained loyal to democratic principles; in December 1870, Palacký's son-in-law, F. L. Rieger, protested openly and in the name of the Czech people against the German seizure of Alsatia-Lothringia and proclaimed his sympathies for French democracy.

Naturally their sincerity of principle did not win sympathy for the Czechs at the conservative Hapsburg court. But even the court, with its allies the landowners, was being overshadowed by the German Liberals and had to ask for help from the Slavonic nations. New imperial pledges alternated with proclamations of states of emergency and open support to the German minority in Bohemia and Moravia who were in control in these lands against all logic and in defiance of the Czech majority. The passivity of Czech politicians indirectly supported this state of affairs. At one time the Germans of Bohemia controlled the whole Austrian Parliament. This was when in protest the Czechs, Poles, Italians, Slovenes and Ukrainians had recalled their representatives. Making use of circumstances which had led the Czechs into a blind alley, the Germans in Bohemia got into the habit of using and misusing their political position, which in fact was not theirs. After the economic debacle of 1873, when a wave of anti-Semitism swept Austria, marking the birth of pan-Germanism, the Germans in Bohemia became its stalwart supporters. When from time to time the conservative court needed the support of the Slavonic members of Parliament and tried gradually to introduce a more just plebiscite, the leaders of the Germans in Bohemia took the attitude that "their votes must not only be counted, but that they should be weighed as well and treated accordingly". They did not want parity on a national basis; they wanted a majority and they did not hesitate to exercise against their Czech fellow-citizens the worst abuses.

Thus, while Austria was willy-nilly on the way to political liberalism and democracy, the Germans in Bohemia and Moravia were fighting a losing battle. In 1878 the crisis in the Balkans showed clearly the inner divisions in the monarchy. The Czechs and Southern Slavs felt sympathy towards the Serbs, Bulgarians and Russians. Of course, they were in a minority. The foreign policy of Austria-Hungary, traditionally executed by the Hungarian noblemen, bore the obsolete ship of the monarchy into the stormy seas of Balkan intrigue. Slowly Austria-Hungary was becoming a spearhead of German expansion into the Middle East. The military occupation of Bosnia and Herzegovina, unsympathetic as it was to the Slavonic nations, strengthened their position inside the monarchy. Large numbers of Czech soldiers, engineers, merchants and scientists left for the Balkans, and through their activity there created new links between these countries and their homeland. From the 70's of the nineteenth century there were always Czechs in Belgrade and Sofia, helping to organize the new states.

On the other hand, the situation in Slovakia grew worse and worse. The Slovak stress on their linguistic individuality and their independence from the rebellious Czechs did not help. From 1874 (to the end of World War I) the Slovaks had no secondary schools, their national societies were being prohibited, their poets were growing to be addicts of mysticism and frustration.

The economic development of Austria-Hungary was slowly transforming the Czech lands into the leading industrial area. A considerable part of industry was already controlled by the Czechs. The power of the landowners was decreasing as the Czechs were building up their own capital. Even more remarkable than their material wealth was their technical skill and high standard of education.

From 1882 a new academic generation was going out from a Czech University of Prague (up to that time German – now divided into two parts). Among the teaching staff of the university, T. G. Masaryk, a young reader in philosophy soon became widely known. Descended from a family of Slovak peasants, he had been for some time a village blacksmith's apprentice, and he became a self-made man and a professor. He started his lectures with a survey of English philosophy because he saw the perils of the fashionable German teaching. On an English model he founded the "Athenaeum" magazine in Prague, and in it he began his fight against the romantic and popular falsifications of Czech history. He became famous for his courageous stand against anti-Semitism, and soon he was the recognized representative of an active group of Czech intellectuals.

Masaryk's stand against anti-Semitism revealed another chasm between Czechs and Germans. In Austria the latter had just discovered a leader in G. Schönerer, the inventor of a teaching shared by Gobi-

Early designs for the Sokol uniform
Drawings by the Czech painter Josef Mánes

neau, Houston Chamberlain and finally by Adolf Hitler. Schönerer thought little of Austria and believed in Greater Germany, the superiority of the German race and the lesser value of the Slavs. The pioneers of Schönerer's ideas were the Germans from Bohemia, especially students, who liked to terrorize the Prague streets.

German provocation did not fail to bring a fierce reaction from the Czechs, who were Francophile. The Czechs built the Prague National Theatre and saw in it the realization of part of their national programme, and organized the Ethnographic Exhibition as an expression of the programme of pan-Slavism. No wonder that German provocation was followed by Czech demonstrations, directed against the dynasty as well. In 1894 the situation was especially critical; special measures were used by the military government in Bohemia. A group of Czech youth, called Omladina (Youth), was brought before a special court and sentenced to long terms of imprisonment. Many future politicians and leaders of workers' organizations were among the condemned.

New divisions began to disintegrate Czech society; a social consciousness was among the most important of them. The importance of the old political representatives of the Czech nation was decreasing, the ideas of liberalism and nationalism ceased to be of topical importance. New political parties appeared, based on the awakened class feeling. Social democracy came to the front, as soon as the working classes got their voting rights. Masaryk's Realist Party, though still not numerous, became representative of the progressive intelligentsia of Bohemia and Moravia, but it had its followers in Slovakia as well, thus forming another link between the two nations.

In vain did the German historian Mommsen proclaim, that "the Czech skull was not responsive to reason, but that blows would bring it to understanding", adding that these blows would fall in the forthcoming struggle between the two nationalities "in a struggle of life and death". In vain did the Germans of Bohemia advocate the division of Bohemia into two separate regions. The world was changing while their policy remained that of the declining bourgeois nationalism. The Russian Revolution of 1905 turned the working classes into radicals and the politicians of Austria gave the franchise to all adults, thus fulfilling the old Czech request. Had it come earlier, this act could have changed the course of events. Thus the reform and the elections of 1907 did little to influence the structure of the Dual Monarchy. Social problems were already desperately interwoven with the problems of nationalities.

The most dangerous situation was that of Hungary and the border-regions, inhabited by Yugoslavs. The Magyar rulers of the country frustrated constitutional reforms and proceeded to liquidate the Slovak political leaders. Thus the year 1907 is the year of the massacre of 17 Slovak people at the village of Černová. Two years later the lands of Bosnia and Herzegovina were annexed to the monarchy against the will of the inhabitants. The annexation led to a new strain between Austria and Serbia. In the Croatian capital of Zagreb the Austrians brought to trial the political leaders of the Yugoslav population. This gave Professor Masaryk an opportunity to help the accused, skilfully throwing light on the unscrupulous methods of the Austrian government's proceedings. Masaryk's defence of the Croats in the Viennese Parliament was a more eloquent witness to Slavonic friendship than the Slavonic Congress, called to Prague by the heir of Czech political liberalism, Dr Karel Kramář.

In 1914, the dead tree of the Austro-Hungarian monarchy was ripe to fall. For the last sixty years of its existence it had been a living anachronism, as it had no reason for existence after 1867. It had no political programme and its government was capable of holding in check the rebellious nationalities only as far as peace prevailed in Europe. A military conflict was sure to show the abysmal differences between the attitude of the ruling nations; Germans and Magyars, and the nations dominated, especially the Slavonic nations. The Czech nation was entering a new period of European history much better equipped than it had been during the crisis of 1848. It was better organized, better educated, and it was not without allies. Above all, the Czechs, whose activities in 1848 had been so much behind those of their Hungarian and German neighbours, had succeeded in using the time. A German newspaperman, writing about the situation of the Czechs in 1914 summed up: "The Slavs today are democrats by conviction while the Germans try to stop progress. Having thrown away the ballast of aristocracy, the Czechs were able to unite the whole nations, the working classes in the first line. The Czechs are fighting for democracy, the Germans for privilege."

XII

THE FIGHT FOR NATIONAL FREEDOM

The outbreak of the first World War in July 1914 was the result of the tension between Vienna and Belgrade. It is not uninteresting to mention that a year earlier T. G. Masaryk had gone to Belgrade, and returned with Serbian suggestions for the improving of relations between both the states. The government of Austria-Hungary let this occasion pass without notice. The immediate pretext for the declaration of war on Serbia was the assassination of the imperial successor to the Austro-Hungarian throne, Francis Ferdinand. In Bohemia he was known as an adherent of federalism, but at the same time as a supporter of the plans of the German Emperor, William II, and as a rigid autocrat and bigoted Catholic. So Czech public opinion, with its democratic, Slavonic and often anti-clerical tendencies, was in no way disturbed by the assassination. But the war against Serbia and Russia, two countries to which the sympathies of a very great part of the nation were bound, was regarded as an evil only a little lesser than civil war.

The very beginning of the last war-adventure of the Hapsburg monarchy was accompanied by the suppression of all political freedom. The Austro-Hungarian government embarked on a struggle, which from a preventive campaign in the Balkans turned to a world-war of two power-groups, without Parliament and without a free press. Czech politicians took, roughly, two standpoints in this situation. K. Kramář, the representative of Czech Liberalism and Neoslavism, was for the Czech nation's remaining passive, reckoning that the Russian Army would in any case sooner or later occupy Bohemia and that they would probably put on the throne one of the Romanov dynasty.

R. W. Seton-Watson

T. G. Masaryk too believed that the surety for Czech and Slovak freedom could only be the support of Russia, guaranteed by a common frontier, but he knew only too well the weaknesses of the Czarist régime, which after all had prohibited his book "Russia and Europe". Masaryk therefore defended political action even in the West, and was not satisfied with passivity either at home or abroad. Czech intellectuals identified themselves from the very start much more with Masaryk than with Kramář; and among them were the first victims of the High Command's authoritarian regime established in Těšín.

By the end of the year 1914 Masaryk had already established contact with his friends abroad, i. e. with the English publicists, Wickham Steed and Seton Watson, old friends of the Czechs and Slovaks. At home a secret organisation of internal resistance, the so-called Maffia, began to form itself, and events on the Russian and Serbian front showed that the Czech and Slovak regiments had no wish to fight against other Slavs.

The result was a persecution which led to the arrest of thousands of Czech people, and many "arch-traitors" were sentenced to death, K. Kramář at their head. T. G. Masaryk was warned in time, and remained abroad, protected by a Serbian passport. London became his residence, while two of his disciples worked in Paris, the Lecturer of Sociology, Dr Edward Beneš, one of the founders of the Maffia at home, and the Slovak astronomer, Milan R. Štefánik.

The celebration of the anniversary of John Hus's death in Swiss Geneva on the 6th of July, 1915 marked the official beginning of Czech resistance. There T. G. Masaryk and the French historian, Ernest Denis, recalled the Czech Reformation to justify the new fight for freedom.

In November of the same year the Czechoslovak Committee was established, proclaiming as its goal the achievement of independence. In February, 1916, this Committee became the Czechoslovak National Council, whose President was T. G. Masaryk, Secretary Edward Beneš, and one of the chief collaborators, M. R. Štefánik. The Yugoslav Committee, with the Polish and Rumanian organisation abroad, became its chief allies.

The goal which the representatives of Czechoslovak resistance abroad had proclaimed was by no means easy. The foreign public knew nothing of the old Czech State, long ago absorbed by Germany and

Austria. Few people in France or England were acquainted with Central European problems. Italian mistrust of a united Yugoslavia paralysed potential sympathies there. Russian pan-Slavism succeeded in establishing the first foreign military unit, the so-called "Czech Group", (Česká družina) but it suffered on the one hand from mistrust of the Czechs in governing circles and on the other from the definite monarchic tendency of the movement itself. The U. S. A., home of hundreds of thousands of Czech and Slovak emigrants, remained for a long time neutral.

Nevertheless, the year 1916 marks the overcoming of the first difficulties and the achievement of the first successes. Greatest of these was the acceptance on the list of Allied war aims of liberation of the Italians, Slavs (i. e. Yugoslavs), Rumanians and Czechoslovaks. That success was chiefly the fruit of Dr Beneš's labour; in Paris in the same year he published a book with the uncompromising title: "Détruisez l'Autriche-Hongrie" – "Destroy Austria-Hungary"!

The centre of war-operations, in 1915 confined by a war of positions, moved to the Western Front in France, while the situation in Russia became more and more grave. The entry of Rumania into the war on the side of the Allies led to the establishing of a unified German-Austro-Hungarian command which bound the Hapsburg monarchy wholly to the Emperor William II's war-plans. At the end of 1916 Francis Joseph I died, and his successor Charles took over his inheritance in such a hopeless situation that the voice of the people speedily gave him the title, "The Last". Charles's accession meant a relaxation of terror and an amnesty for Czech prisoners, and led to the assembly of Parliament and inevitable loosening of political control, which finally brought attempts for a separate peace. On the other hand, Charles was forced at his coronation to compromise his freedom of decision, which in the question of Hungary came to be fatal.

The last Parliament of the dynasty assembled in May 1917, in a very disturbed situation. In Russia the Czar régime had fallen and the new government was much more ready to support Czechoslovak resistance. With the end of the Czar's absolutism and America cooperating more and more with the Allies, the democratic cause was strengthened. The Socialist Conference in Stockholm led the socialist leaders to be better informed; they witnessed the first hunger-rebellions, brutally suppressed especially by Hungarian units. Austria-Hungary's situation was so bad that the Foreign Minister, Count Czernin, advised negotiating for a separate peace. The danger that Czech delegates might support the declining monarchy and counteract foreign resistance was put out of consideration with the courageous manifesto of Czech writers in May 1917. Here the claim to fight for their independence was openly expressed. Under the influence of this manifesto, Czech delegates declared themselves in Parliament against the war. They emphasised their claims for freedom and their sympathies for the Russian revolution. The Slovene Korošec made a corresponding declaration for the Yugoslav delegates. No wonder that these declarations brought an expression of indignation from the German and Hungarian side.

At this time Masaryk was on tour in Russia, where the Czechoslovak legions, at last organised on a large scale, won a great success in the Battle of Zborov on July 3rd 1917, in the offensive of General Brusilov. The ill success of the Italians at Caporetto led their goverment to a more conciliatory attitude toward the organisation of Czechoslovak fighting units, the formation of which was also approved in France. The political aim of this army abroad was best expressed by T. G. Masaryk, who wished to create in Russia "a Czech army in the spirit of Czech democracy, but definitely Russophile and conscious of its aim".

Such an army had good hope for a successful existence and an active fight even in the heated soil of weakening Russia. Czechoslovak legionaries, with a feeling for social questions already gained at home, joined in greeting the coming of the November Revolution. Defending the Ukraine against German agressors, Czechoslovak legions shed blood at the side of the forces of the Russian Revolution in their second memorable battle, at Ukrainian Bachmač. When the weak Russia was forced to peace at Brest-Litovsk, a peace cruelly dictated by the German army, Czech leaders with Masaryk at their head realised that now the Czechoslovak forces had nothing to gain in Russia. Masaryk therefore, before leaving Russia himself, arranged for the departure of the Czechoslovak forces across Siberia to the Western Front. With his rare gift for arriving in the right place at the right time, Masaryk set off for America who had now taken over the political initiative. On the 8th of January 1918, at a time when the Prague streets were full of demonstrating workers who had found their leader in Vl. Tusar and others who understood the importance of the time, President Wilson proclaimed his 14 points. A Congress of "suppressed nationalities" met in Rome two months later, further proof, if it was needed, of the wish of the Central European conquered nations to leave the monarchy. The resistance movement at home had a great success in the formulation of the so-called "Twelfth Night Agreement", where demands were raised for the future unification of Bohemia, Moravia, Silesia and Slovakia. A further success was the second entry of Czech writers into politics, when they formulated a national vow, put forward on the 13th April in Prague by Alois Jirásek. The poet Jaroslav Kvapil, seized the occasion of the celebrations to commemorate the jubilee of the Prague National Theatre to make a pronouncement for Czechoslovak unity, self-development of nations and unity with other Slav nations. Even the Slovaks, fighting a desperate battle, declared themselves on the 24th of May in Turčanský Sv. Martin for union with the Czechs. The Czechoslovak National Council was recognised during that year by France, Britain, U. S. A. and Italy as the representative of the nation.

The spring of the same year (1918) saw a dangerous tension between some of the representatives of the Red Army and the Czechoslovak legions. On the encouragement of L. Trockij an attempt was made to hold up the march of the legions. It is characteristic that J. V. Stalin stood up at the time against Trockij's attempts. For a time there existed the danger, that reactionary forces in Russia and the conservatives among the Allied leaders would try to use the legions to foster civil war. This danger was removed, by the wisdom of Masaryk and Beneš on the one hand and that of the Czech soldiers on the other, for they refused to be brought to the level of a mercenary army fighting for foreign interests. In the end the whole struggle had not such fatal consequences as might have been expected. The evacuation of the legions across Siberia was made secure, and the legionaries came to an even greater understanding of the social problems of the growing and strengthening Soviet Union.

Masaryk's activities in America met with overwhelming success. The Philadelphia Hall of Independence was the place where the wish of the Czechoslovak people was proclaimed to set up their own democracy and to leave the Hapsburg monarchy, which from the middle of September openly negotiated for peace. The collapse of the Balkan front at the end of September finished the German dream of conquering Europe. On the 18th October the Allies recognised the Czechoslovak National Council as the first government, and at the same time President Wilson, in his reply to the Austro-Hungarian offer of peace, informed the diplomats of the monarchy that they should negotiate directly with the representatives of Czechoslovaks and Yugoslavs. Andrássy, the last Austro-Hungarian Foreign Minister, accepted even this condition on the 27th of October; it meant the end of the monarchy.

The Prague National Council, composed of the representatives of all leading political groups, Socialist as well as Catholic, effected the change of government on the 28th October 1918 and took over power without bloodshed. A day later the Slovaks, whose representative Dr V. Šrobár, another of Masaryk's disciples, became a member of the Prague National Council, declared in Turčanský Sv. Martin that the "Slovak nation is both by language and history a part of a united Czechoslovak nation" and pronouced its claim for a common state. T. G. Masaryk, elected as first President of the democratic Czechoslovak Republic, returned to Prague on the 21st December 1918; in his first message to the nation he began by reciting the words of the great exile, J. Amos Comenius, which are so full of faith that the governance of things would again return to the hands of his conquered nation. Over the gulf of 300 years began a new era of building the state.

XIII

THE BUILDING OF THE STATE

The builders of the Czechoslovak State had by the gift of fate a stretch of twenty years in which to do their creative work. At her birth this state was given certain characteristics which were to direct her future life. She arose out of the will of the Czech and Slovak people, through the union of the "historic" Czech lands (divided from West to East into Bohemia, Moravia and Silesia) – forming the centre of the state – and the more easterly Slovakia. By the will of the Ukrainians abroad as well as of the population at home, Carpathian Ruthenia joined them, and was incorporated in summer 1919 as an autonomous whole. After the destruction of independent Ukraine she looked to Czechoslovakia for support. Only in South Slovakia did the frontiers of the new state differ a little from those frontiers which from historical experience had proved to be the best for the maintenance of political independence. Inside the frontiers of the Czechoslovak State there remained a little more than three million Germans and half a million Hungarians. The new state was ready to make an agreement about minorities immediately after the declaration of the peace treaties. The constitution was proclaimed in the name of the people in 1920; in agreement with foreign commentators, we can truthfully declare that the Czechoslovak democratic constitution, in contrast with others, was a really living constitution, even when Czechoslovakia was the only democracy east of the Rhine. It was characterised by a real social feeling, which appeared in the great social system, unparalleled in Central Europe, and in many respects ahead of social legislation in the Western democracies. The social feeling and the popular basis were after all evident from the fact that the men guiding the Republic were men who worked with hands and with head – intellectuals, farmers and workers.

Czechoslovakia effected a political democracy, but had no time to effect an economic democracy as well. No wonder, for in the year 1918 German capital was fully 60% of the whole, landed property was still very largely in the hands of a foreign aristocracy and even after the agrarian reforms was alien to the people, in the hands of a narrow class of landowners.

Meanwhile the extension of the frontiers of the new state was not achieved without some opposition. In summer 1919 the Hungarian government made an attack on South Slovakia which was beaten off only with real difficulty. Though the Peace of Trianon stabilized the frontiers, the political situation in Hungary did not change; Horthy was declaring himself for revisionism and had no interest in seeking agreement with a so-called "usurping" republic. A similar conflict occurred over Těšín, where there were in 1920 233,000 Poles, 115,000 Czechs and 76,000 Germans. The district had been occupied by both states, roughly along the natural frontiers supplied by the river Olza; there remained on the Czechoslovak side the Karviná coalfields, essential for the maintenance of industry in the district of Moravská Ostrava, and a railway line of vital importance, leading from Silesia to East Slovakia, the only usable railway connecting with East Slovakia at this time and a link with the greater part of the Czech population. Czechoslovakia proposed a plebiscite for the whole region, under international supervision, but more and more unpleasant incidents occurred till in the end the Foreign Ministers of both States – Beneš and Grabski, – applied for arbitration. The same month a commission of the great powers decided upon a frontier, which left the majority of Poles in Poland and the majority of Czechs in Czechoslovakia. Dr Beneš's decision was not popular, for public opinion in Silesia was convinced that a plebiscite would have brought greater territorial gains. The ancient duchy was thus divided, but the Poles were not satisfied either and later explained Czechoslovak unwillingness to give in to Poland with the comment that the sympathies of Czechoslovakia were with Russia, against whom Poland was then fighting.

The German minority in Bohemia and Moravia was not at the time willing to recognise the new state of affairs. But it is characteristic that none of their leaders thought of uniting with neighbouring Germany.

In the beginning four so-called governments were appointed in the frontier districts, which should have had and actually had no contacts with each other, still less with Austria, to whom these "governments" reported. This region, called Deutschböhmen (Sudetenland was the correct geographical name for only the Moravian-Silesian part, where the region of Sudetenland lies), did not form a unit and was very quickly and without opposition occupied by the Czechoslovak forces formed abroad. At the time the French Premier was more resolute in refusing territorial advances to Germany than the Czechoslovak Foreign Minister. The bitterness of the German minority abated with time, when in the midst of the German and Austrian chaos the new state offered economic advantages and the German minority itself proposed only a partial transfer, unwilling to reduce her power in the state. Despite disagreements over the fate of Deutschböhmen, relations between Czechoslovakia and Austria were good, and it really could not be otherwise in two countries related both by economic bonds and ties of blood. But they were strained from time to time by attempts to unite Austria and Germany, and that considerably. It was clear to everyone that an Anschluss would have most fatal effects for Czechoslovak independence.

A second danger threatened the state, that the Hapsburgs might return. This danger and Hungarian revisionism led to a greater friendship towards the now neighbouring Rumania and the united Yugoslavia. In the years 1920–21 the three states formed the so-called "Little Entente", a defensive organisation directed against the Hapsburgs, which proved its usefulness in 1921 when "Charles the Last" made his last attempt to return to Hungary. As long as there were monarchic circles in power in Hungary, pro-German circles in Austria and anti-Soviet circles in Poland, there was to Czech deep disappointment little hope of starting closer contacts with these states, although both the economic and the political situation would have encouraged such a federation. Apart from the Little Entente, Czechoslovak independence was supported by the treaty of alliance with France. This country directed European politics during that fateful interval when the United States became isolationist and Great Britain was again attempting to foster the balance of power by indirect support of Italy and in the end even of Germany, while the Soviet Union battled at home for social rebirth. All the more reason why Czechoslovakia with the greater faith and sincerity took part in building the League of Nations, in this way demonstrating its traditional strength of spirit, and preferring to cooperate for peace rather than prepare for war.

Yet despite all difficulties, the builders of the state had much success during the first ten years. Development at home was extraordinarily peaceful. In the 1920 election the Socialists had a narrow victory over the bourgeois parties and the result was an Agrarian-Socialist coalition. In 1925 came narrow victory for the bourgeois parties and the government coalition was formed without Socialists but with the representatives of the German minority; this semed to prove indubitably that the Germans had accepted the status quo, i. e. the existence of the Republic. In 1927 the Socialists regained their strength and reappeared in the government. The Czechoslovak system of having numerous parties of varying shades of opinion encouraged the formation of coalitions, which made impossible sudden radical changes and assured stability of political development.

In the late twenties this stability of development came to an end; the industrial regions of the frontier, inhabited by the German minority, and which depended on export were heavily hit. The economic crisis made itself felt even in Slovakia, where the government had built up an educational system, such as the Slovak people had not known till then. In the new Slovak schools there grew up a generation of intellectuals who sorely needed a field of activity and complained that official posts were to a large extent monopolised by Czechs. This of course had come about because of the scarcity of educated Slovaks – in 1918 there were only between 750 and 1000. The Catholic People's Party, under Andrej Hlinka, who represented a type of conservative clerical no longer to be found in Bohemia or Moravia, won the support of the dissatisfied under the watchword "Slovak Autonomy". The party lost prestige, however, with the revelation of Hlinka's dependency on the arch-traitors, V. Tuka and Š. Mach, who endangered the safety of the Republic by foreign intrigue. After losing the elections, Hlinka left the government and formulated even more radical demands, the more so when his Protestant rival, M. Hodža, attained the office of Prime Minister.

Meanwhile out of the economic crisis Hitler's movement was growing in Germany and beginning to endanger the whole of Central Europe. In 1933 Hitler came to power and at once put pressure upon

Austria. The Chancellor Dolfuss fell a victim to him, and an Austrian Anschluss was only prevented by Mussolini, who was still dreaming of dominating in Central Europe himself. The same year saw the death of the Yugoslav King Alexander and the French Foreign Minister Barthou, at the hands of assassins in the pay of Italy. The use of brute force in politics had far-reaching results. With the passage of time and under the influence of the ruling clique, Yugoslavia was excluded from the politics of Central Europe; France found no one along the followers of Barthou able to take over his political legacy and bring her Central European allies, Poland and Czechoslovakia, into one line. Instead, the Polish government began a selfish and blinded policy of official friendship with Germany. Finally Mussolini used his influence to prevent greater trust developing among the Central European states; the Pact of Rome, signed with Austria and Hungary, created a counter-bloc to the Little Entente, already weakened by King Carol's authoritarian rule.

The only Central European politician who foresaw the danger was Dr Beneš; in the year 1933 he had already declared in an interview that Adolf Hitler wanted to seize Austria and Czechoslovakia, occupy Danzig and crush Poland. So he tried to lessen the threat of danger from Nazi Germany by applying the principle of collective security within the frame of the League of Nations; and he declared that this international organisation would be strengthened by the entry of the Soviet Union. When France negotiated an alliance with the Soviet Union, he put through a similar alliance between Czechoslovakia and the Soviet Union, effected on the 16th May 1935.

The same year President Masaryk, then eighty-five years old, resigned from office (he died September 14th 1937), and was succeeded by Dr Beneš. "States are maintained by the very ideals which brought them into being" had been the message of the President-Liberator. And the democratic ideals of Czechoslovakia were threatened by an enemy of the most dangerous character, by its German citizens. As early as 1918 a party was founded in Bohemia under the name of the German Workers' National Socialist Party (N. S. D. A. P.), recruiting its members among the Pan-German and Czech-baiting Radicals. This party represented a small fraction of the German minority, and it did not gain more members later, when it became influenced by the Viennese Professor, Othmar Spann, and started irredentist activity. In 1933 the party was dissolved by its leaders. Its heritage was taken over only a year later, when Konrad Henlein, up to that time a modest teacher of gymnastics and one of the leaders of the German union of gymnasts (Turners), founded the so-called Sudeten-German Home Front. Othmar Spann was soon replaced by Adolf Hitler, and the teaching of the National Union (Volksgemeinschaft) became the new Gospel, preached from pulpits, in political meetings and in schools. Antisemitic feeling and a hatred for the Czechs poisoned the life in the border-regions. For a long time the Czech bourgeois parties saw in Henlein an ally against the Socialists. The ageing Dr Kramář even expressed his gratitude for the growth of Fascism in Italy. So were the police not allowed to interfere with the meeting of Herr Henlein's followers and thus, thanks partly to the reign of terror, his party came out of the elections of 1935 with a remarkable success. Henlein's party got 66% of all German votes and thus encouraged changed its title into that of the Sudeten German Party (Sudetendeutsche Partei).

Under the threat of imminent danger fortifications were being built in the border-regions. Many Germans were employed in this way, and the economic crisis also slowly overcome. The grievances of social oppression were accordingly replaced by grievances of civic and especially cultural oppression. At that time the German minority had three schools of university standard and 3–5% of German school-children attended non-German schools. It was notorious that German fathers were sending their children for shorter periods to Czech schools to give them opportunity to learn Czech but some sections of public opinion abroad were willing to listen to the German grievances, and from 1935 on Herr Heinlein several times visited England. Personally he was not at all radical – abroad he advocated totalitarian ideas and the struggle with Communism, and both of these appealed to the feeling of a powerful section of the British Conservative party. Some of Henlein's colleagues, especially his adjutant, K. H. Frank, were much more outspoken. In March 1941 Henlein showed his true face boastfully when he spoke at a Nazi rally in Vienna. According to him then, the political aim of the S. D. P. had consisted from the beginning in the destruction of Czechoslovakia because Czechoslovakia formed an obstacle to German plans, and therefore she was to perish by all means.

By that time Czechoslovakia was well on her guard, and on the 21st of May 1938 when Hitler wanted to repeat his tactics – successful

The Sokol Festival of 1938

in Austria – he was faced with a Czech mobilisation. As France, and probably Great Britain as well, approved the Czech attitude, Hitler had to retreat and try other tactics. His London friends were successful in influencing the Prime Minister, Mr. Chamberlain. After the conclusion of the Sokol festival, which showed the vitality of Czechoslovak-Yugoslav friendship and the national will to defence, a British visitor came to Prague. Lord Runciman came over as mediator and investigator. His mediatory and investigatory activities were carefully influenced by his hosts and friends, recruited from the German nobility and the Sudeten German party.

At the same time the initiative was won by Mr. Chamberlain, who got rid of the Foreign Secretary Mr. Eden and did not care for the opinions of the Foreign Office either. Events were then succeeding each other in swift sequence. The British mediator, Lord Runciman, advocated the secession of the Czechoslovak border regions, inhabited mainly by the Germans. The so-called Anglo-French plan, sketched on September 21st went even farther, and foresaw the cession of all the districts with 50% of German population. On the night of September 22nd soon after midnight the ministers of France and the United Kingdom submitted this plan in an ultimative form to the President of the Republic. The French minister went as far as threaten that Czechoslovakia would become guilty of the war, if she did not yield. Great Britain was, of course, in no way pledged to help Czechoslovakia, but Czech public opinion took her for the representative of European democracy. France flagrantly broke her pledge of alliance and was nearly assuming the attitude of an enemy. President Beneš had the promise of the Soviet Union, by alliance bound to help only if France did the same, that it would help under all conditions. He was however aware, that this would mean the excuse for a "Holy War" against Communist U.S.S.R. and its Czechoslovak ally. Having considered this the government yielded to the dictate and handed in its resignation.

Mr. Chamberlain then started for Godesberg, only to discover to his surprise, that the conditions of the Anglo-French plan were no longer acceptable to Germany. For a while even Mr. Chamberlain seemed to lose his patience. The Prague government was advised from London to mobilize. The mobilisation was greeted with satisfaction, even enthusiasm in all districts of the Republic. President Roosevelt made a speech too, and warned Hitler against the use of force. After the calm of a few days Hitler started a new wave of blackmail and on September 28th, in the middle of a speech in the House of Commons, Mr. Chamberlain announced his intention to depart for Munich. There, on Sept. 29th, Hitler and Mussolini met Chamberlain and Daladier, and the Czechoslovak delegates were presented with the map of areas to be ceded. The Munich dictate, enforced by the four powers and set up by Hitler, was never acknowledged by the Czechoslovak Parliament, which according to the constitution alone had the right to approve the territorial changes. With the protective belt of frontier-mountains Czechoslovakia lost the warrant of her independence. This was clear as early as October 7th, when the evacuation of the ceded territories was concluded. In these "German" territories there remained about one million Czechs, and thousands of German anti-Fascists, delivered by the British and French to death and concentration-camps. With the destruction of the Czechoslovak state Central Europe had its spine broken, the Western democracies lost more than 40 divisions of potential allies, and Germany had no obstacle in her march to the South-East.

The example of predatory Nazism was followed by the régimes of Poland and Hungary. With unbelievable shortsightedness and selfishness Poland occupied the Těšín area, inhabited by 77.000 Poles, 20.000 Germans and 132.000 Czechs. Thousands of Czechs were soon expelled from the Polish occupation zone in a way very similar to that of the Germans. In November the so-called Vienna Agreement handed over the extensive areas of Southern and Eastern Slovakia to the Hungary of Admiral Horthy, who entered the Slovak town of Košice on horseback, with great pomp.

On October 5th President Beneš was forced to resign and soon afterwards left the country on his way to exile. His office was taken over by the President of the Highest Court of Administration, Dr Emil Hácha. He was installed thanks to the pressure exerted by the new Prime Minister, Rudolph Beran, who was known to have been for years in close contact with the followers of Henlein. The agony and moral stress under which the rump – Czechoslovakia lay in the winter of 1938–39 was brought to an end by another brutal act of Hitler's. This time Hitler used the blindfolded Slovak chauvinists instead of the German separatists. At the beginning of March 1939 Beran, encouraged by Berlin, took measures against the Slovak radicals led by Tiso. Then Hitler intervened, after a farcical invitation, sent by Tiso to the "protector" of the Slovak nation. On March 14th Tiso and his accomplices Tuka and Mach proclaimed the "free state of Slovakia" by Hitler's will. The same evening Hácha was called to Berlin, and under the threat of a bloody invasion was asked to sign a proclamation, putting the Czech nation under the protection of its worst enemy. It is unnecessary to lay stress on the fact that Hácha had no constitutional right to sign such a document. After all, the German troops did not wait for the conclusion of unnecessary formalities and started on March 14th to occupy Bohemia and Moravia. The next day, on his return to Prague, Hácha found in the Prague Castle his new master, Adolf Hitler. He had come to Prague to proclaim the transformation of the occupied Czech territory into the first German Protectorate. German police, Gestapo and informers were in Prague, too. The final test of the Czech will to live was beginning.

The Occupation: Freiherr Neurath at Prague Castle

XIV

THE ULTIMATE ORDEAL

If we pronounce the years 1938–1945 the years of trial for Czechs and Slovaks in their will to live, then we do not exaggerate. The second World War touched the very roots of their being, moral and physical, and brought the country suffering as great as it had probably ever experienced in its history.

The bitter trial started at the very beginning of the occupation. Only in the moral sphere did the occupation bring light, for many an undecided and uprooted man saw immediately that now had come a struggle for the very existence of the nation, that it was no longer possible to listen to the luring sounds of a hostile ideology. Popular instinct realised from the reaction of world opinion to the occupation that Hitler had entered on a course which would lead him into the abyss. Meanwhile there was little to be heard about German plans as the police system was not yet built up. The Germans were busy with preparations against Poland in which they made use of the neighbouring Moravian plain. To check doubtful Czech nationals, the Germans used from the very beginning members of the German minority, which became by a special decree German citizens, whilst the Czechs were only members, hirelings in their own house, and that temporarily, for of this the Germans made no secret.

The reaction was an outburst of national awareness, which showed itself in passive resistance, in passengers' boycotting trams, in sober celebrations of the poet Mácha, whose remains were transferred from Litoměřice to Prague before the Germans entered. From the start there grew up in the land a net of secret organisations which tried to keep up contact with the countries abroad to which daily hundreds of young men were fleeing. On the 1st of September the Germans started their first action against the Czechs. Thousands of hostages were arrested at the beginning of the war with Poland and dragged to a concentration camp in Dachau. As the hostages were selected from the leading intellectual circles, the resulting loss was great. Dr Hácha intervened again and again in the following months and begged for the release of at least a part of them. The Germans did not immediately reject the request, and several weeks later released one of the hostages, thinking that the prisoners' families might break down under the strain and coquetting with them in their attempts to free the prisoners. The 28th October 1939 became a day of great manifestation of the Czech faith that their freedom would be restored. Prague became the centre of incidents, blood flowed, and reports of a failing German organisation went out into the world. At all costs the Germans wished to forestall such reports; they put the blame for the conspiracy on the university students; the night of 17th November saw the occupation of the colleges and the arrest of thousands of students, some of whom were dragged to concentration camp in Oranienburg, some tortured and dispelled. The brutal Germans, led by the so-called State-Secretary Frank, who guarded "the Protector" Neurath, chose ten or so of the leading members of the student body as the executioners' target, taking no account of their political opinions.

After the end of the Polish campaign, the régime became more and more tyrannous, whilst the number of collaborants among the Germans of Bohemia grew. These were blinded by the prospect of material advantages and the evident success of the Hitler régime. Former friends became spies, informers, nay, even executioners. Controllers were chosen from among them to censor the press and to suppress Czech books, thousands of which disappeared in flames. The German inspectors of Czech schooling took care to ravage the property of the Czech universities which had been closed, to reduce the number of Czech schools to a third, to wipe out Czech schools in the Sudetenland and gradually to transform all schools into German ones. All activity of sport organisations, at the head of which was Sokol, was stopped; all churches, without distinction, were persecuted, for the spirit is dangerous to barbarism. Moreover the property of the inhabitants of Bohemia and Moravia was confiscated or administered by German occupants, whether under the pretence of political distrust or racial hatred.

The effect of the first wave of terror was on the whole small. The people followed the return of President Beneš into Europe, as well as the cold welcome which the French gave to our resistance movement, which for the protection of the French was building its first units in autumn 1939. The old bitterness lasted till spring 1940, when against all hope even of the opponents of our ally – for the French had betrayed us – France collapsed; the Czechoslovak units escaped to England thanks to British help, but by a hair's breadth and with tremendous losses.

For some time everyone at home felt heavy at heart – the invasion of the British Isles was threateting at any moment; yet Premier Churchill, who belonged to the few faithful, who saw in Munich a catastrophe, stood firm, although only the Channel, the Navy and a small number of Air Force, including the Czechoslovaks from France, stood between the German panzer armies and the British nation.

Great Britain held out, and became the seat of the Czechoslovak National Committee, who were gaining a much more favourable position than the liberators had had in the years 1914–1918. Czech minds were more at rest, as it became evident that, even though the war would last long, yet its ultimate result would indubitably be victory. The people's revolt in Yugoslavia in March 1941 almost caused a demonstration in Prague, but the persecution which followed, directed against all Czech people who could have had anything to do with the sister nation, was without effect. And when on the 22nd June of the same year, the microphones announced the beginning of the German drive into the Soviet Union, all the people – whether in their homes or local prisons or afar in concentration camps – knew what this signified the end of Hitler's Germany. This knowledge was strengthened by the news, that the Czechoslovak Government with Mgr. Šrámek at its head, had been recognised by the British Government in July, and that the President, Dr Beneš, had negotiated a treaty with Great Britain and Soviet Russia.

Meanwhile a Czechoslovak military unit was being formed in Russia. In August 1942 the British Government declared that they did not feel bound by the Munich Agreement and that they recognised the old Czechoslovak frontiers. At home, the confidence of the Czechs had to be broken, Baron Neurath being recalled for that purpose. And now, on the eve of St. Wenceslas' Day, 22nd September 1941, began

Winston Churchill and President Edvard Beneš
At a review of the Czechoslovak Brigade in Great Britain

the terrible rule of Heydrich. Prime Minister Eliáš, who was trying to lead the government so as to serve the people at home and its representatives abroad, fell victim to Heydrich. Extraordinary courts sent hundreds of patriots to their death, and the Nazi prisons killed further thousands. This time it was the turn of the old politicians, the fighters of the first World War, and the members of the Sokol. This was the time when the Far East saw the treacherous invasion of Pearl Harbour and when Germany declared war on the United States.

The attempt of Heydrich to disintegrate the Czech nation with the help of the quisling Moravec ended with an attack on him in the streets of Prague on the 27th May 1942. Now there appeared on the scene the executioner of the Czech nation, Frank. He, together with the new representative of the old Protector, Daluege, gave orders for the execution, during one month, of 1300 victims chosen at random, but taking good care that the chosen ones might be probable leaders of the resistance. The symbol of the loss to the Czech intelligentsia was the death of the heroic author, Vl. Vančura. The wiping out of the village of Lidice, again chosen almost by chance, shook the conscience of world public opinion. But Lidice was not the only community which fell victim to German hatred. At this time, so-called "historians" from among the local Germans came with the plan of a "revival" of German colonisation of Bohemia and Moravia.

On their advice the German authorities began to clear out, without thought of compensation, large territories in the South of Bohemia, so that they might join other territories evacuated south of Prague and along the Elbe. The little German island near Vyškov in Central Moravia was strengthened at the same time by the clearing out of mountain villages farther to the North.

The cast-out population of the desolated villages wandered to more congenial surroundings. This was happening in the winter months of 1942–43 when the German catastrophes at Stalingrad and in North Africa took place. The United Nations were more and more clearly gaining the upper hand, Germany was threatened with day and night attacks; these killed many a victim among the ranks of the Czech population too, who had been dragged to the Reich. The tale of the fortress of Europe lost all weight after the successful invasion of Italy and the victorious march of the Red Army, with whom at this time a Czechoslovak unit was also fighting. The Czechs distinguished them-

President Beneš visits F. D. Roosevelt in 1942

selves in the Battle of Kiev in autumn 1943, against the same enemy and almost on the same spot where a quarter of a century earlier Czech legions of the first World War had won fame.

Gradually at this time even the Czech and Slovak territories were transforming themselves into a fighting belt; air attacks became more frequent; and in August 1944 a Slovak rising broke out in Banská Bystrica, which showed clearly to the world, that they too, though they had been terrorised by a treacherous clique and by the Germans, were among Hitler's enemies and stood beside their brethren. By the side of Czechs and Slovaks, and British and American specialists, there fought also the Soviet partisans and parachutists, bound together in the common struggle and against ever-threatening death.

Although the Germans were successful in driving the guerillas to the mountains, skirmishes continued in Slovakia, Bohemia and particularly in Moravia until the end of the war. Czechoslovak units fought beside the Soviets for the Carpathian paths – whilst in the West Czechoslovak armoured brigade blockaded the port of Dunkirk, eagerly following the invasion of Normandy. Czechoslovaks were not missing from the other European battlefields (for instance, Yugoslavia and Italy) either, and their compatriots in America were to be found wherever the American forces sped.

In the first months of 1945 Hitler's Germany was nearing its collapse. But the rule of terror was not abating. K. H. Frank spared no threats about the fate of the Czechs nation and in particular of Prague, should a revolt be organised. From January on, there wandered through the Czech lands heartbreaking collections of prisoners of war and prisoners of concentration camps – half-naked, dying with frost and hunger. Meanwhile, the government arrived in sorely tried Slovakia with President Beneš at its head, according to the plans drawn up as early as autumn 1943, during the arrangement of the Czechoslovak-Soviet Alliance in Moscow. The government announced its programme on the 5th of April 1946 in the newly liberated Košice. The Germans were threatened with such internal disintegration that they did not protest against the coming of the Swiss Red Cross, in order to care for the prisoners in the camp of Terezín, where terrible epidemics had broken out. (The Czechoslovak Red Cross had been abolished by the Germans at the beginning of the war. Some of its leaders died in the concentration camps, and the property was stolen.) The sight of these

The Old Town Clock in Prague
A view of the building destroyed by the Germans in 1945

poor victims from the concentration camps, and of the arrogance of the remaining Germans started one of the flames from which burst on 5th May 1945 the fire of the Prague Rising.

The central organisation of the Prague Rising, the Czechoslovak National Council, at the head of which was Professor Albert Pražák, the Professor of Czech literature in the University of Prague, gave the signal for the fight; it broke out simultaneously in Prague and in certain Moravian towns. At this time the American Army was nearing Plzeň, and the Soviet troops were gaining Olomouc in Moravia. The streets of Prague became a battlefield from the 5th to the 9th of May, a battlefield where Czech patriots, almost with their naked hands, held a mighty garrison in check; with the help of barricades they prevented Marshal Schoerner's attempted seizure of the Central town of Prague, and its transformation into a citadel. The Prague Rising, which became a demonstration of the people's fighting ability as well as of their will to fight, cost the lives of thousands of victims, especially as the awaited help, promised by the Allies, was not forthcoming. Among the victims were not only fighters from the barricades, but even innocent civilians dragged out of their houses, and injured women and children, driven under tanks and shot at in houses. Although the military capitulated on the evening of May the 8th, the fight was carried on by the S. S. troopers. In the early hours of the morning of the 9th the first tanks of the Soviet Armies which had raced from Berlin arrived at the northern tip of the town. The victorious fight was over.

On the 10th of May the Government arrived in Prague, and on the 16th the population of that battle-damaged town that was once more free, greeted the victorious return of their President, Dr E. Beneš. The homecoming of the President marked the very peak of victory; now began a new life.

The liberation of the Republic does not end the history of the nation, in the course of which we have seen many a task confronted, and many still confront every Czech and Slovak. Their country is now damaged by war, ravaged by the enemy and despoiled of all its riches. But she has not been bereft of her greatest gift, her hard-working people, who have shown so often in their history that they will not be broken and that they can build up a new life almost from the roots. The population has been oftener faced with the problems of their very life's existence than possibly the majority of European nations. Now it must successfully solve the building-up of a new social and economic structure, the problem of the political unity of Czechs and Slovaks, and the problem of relations with the rest of the world. But there is no question among all Czechoslovaks of the fact that the new Czechoslovakia must be a firm unit. Therefore there is no place for the majority of the German and Hungarian population who in the services of the enemy sold humanity for a few material advantages. With this problem comes that of the economic rebuilding of our nation. An economic democracy must implement the political democracy; thus only will the safety of the people be ensured.

As soon as such an existence has been ensured, Czechs and Slovaks turn their gaze to distant lands, to seek brotherhood with the nations of the world. Because of her geographical position Czechoslovakia has as her very task to support peace and tolerance in the world, and this task she will uphold in the United Nations' Organisation. A contemporary Russian author has compared Czechoslovakia to a tree which stands most erect where winds from two sides blow upon it. The Czechoslovak people have lived and will live between West and East, uniting the respect of the West for man's individuality with the emphasis of the East on the common good, rather than on the selfishness of the individual. All peace-loving nations of the world will always find in them a devoted friend.

NOTE ON BOOKS

For comparison and further study the English reader will find useful the following books, available in his own language:

The oldest short history, still very readable but slight after 1792 is Francis Lützow's *Bohemia* (Everyman's, London 1919).

Of the two books by Czech authors V. Nosek's *The Spirit of Bohemia* (London, 1926) is of lesser value. K. Krofta's *Short. History of Czechoslovakia* (London and Prague, 1935) suffers by the fact that it was written primarily for Czech readers.

Three notable works were published during the last war: R. W. Seton-Watson's *A History of the Czechs and Slovaks* (London, 1943) is the most accessible of them. Professor R. J. Kerner edited the collective work of American scholars, called *Czechoslovakia* (Berkeley and Los Angeles, 1940). S. Harrison Thomson published his *Czechoslovakia in European History* (Princeton) in 1944.

INDEX

NOTE ON CZECH PRONUNCIATION

The Czech is consistently a phonetic tongue, it is pronounced as it is written. Invariably the accent falls on the first syllable, irrespective of the length of the word.

Before Hus's time Czech orthography resembled somewhat that of the present day Polish or Hungarian. By introducing the diacritic mark, Hus did away with groups of consonants such as cz (corresponding to the English ch), sz (corresponding to the English sh). Thus

č is pronounced as ch in cherry,

š as sh in shall,

ž as in j in the Frech word jour,

ř is thought to be the most difficult to pronounce for a non-Czech. The rsh in Pershing approaches the sound though it does not quite express it.

ch is pronounced as in the Scottish loch.

The vowels are pronounced as in Italian. The diacritic mark tends to show the length. Thus

á is pronounced long as in darling,

é as a in care,

í and ý as ee in tree,

ě as ye in yellow.

INDEX

GREAT BRITAIN AND CZECHOSLOVAKIA
A COMPARATIVE CHRONOLOGY

	Great Britain		Czechoslovakia
B. C.	*Celtic* Britain	B. C.	*Celtic* Boii give name to Bohemia
55	Caesar's first invasion of Britain		
	Roman occupation of Britain		Roman "limes" along the Danube
A. D.		A. D.	
123	Completion of Hadrian's Wall	100	Arrival of the *Germanic* tribes
410	*Germanic* invasions start		
		500–600	*Slavonic* tribes appear in the country
	Anglo-Saxon Britain		
597	Augustine introduces Christianity to Anglo-Saxon England		
		623	Samo creates the first Slavonic empire in Central Europe
664	Synod of Whitby		
			Avar invasions
	Danish invasions	800	Charlemagne attempts to subdue the Slavs in Bohemia
		830	Rise of the Realm of Great Moravia
871	Alfred the Great	863	Cyril and Methodius bring Eastern Christianity to Moravia
		900	Great Moravia overthrown by *Magyars* – Rise of Bohemia and victory of Western Christianity
		929	Death of "Good King Wenceslas"
	Golden Age of the Saxons		
1066	Battle of Hastings *Norman Conquest*		
		1085	Vratislav I, first King of Bohemia
1154	Henry II		
		1158	Vladislav, second King of Bohemia
1170	Murder of Thomas à Becket		
	Richard I imprisoned in Austria	1193	Prince Přemysl deposed
		1197	King Přemysl I and his adviser Robert, Bishop of Moravia
		1212	The Golden Bull of Sicily
1215	Magna Charta		
	Henry III		Princess Agnes
	Richard of Cornwall, King of Germany	1278	King Přemysl Otakar II, his ally, dies at Marchfeld

1300 Edward I fights to acquire Wales and Scotland	1300 King Wenceslas II acquires Poland and Hungary 1306 End of the Přemyslids John of Luxemburg
1346 Black Prince wins the Battle of Crécy	1346 Death of King John at Crécy
Hundred Years' War	1348 Charles IV: Prague University founded
1381 Peasants' revolt Richard II Wycliffe in Oxford	1382 Charles' daughter Anna becomes Queen of England – Hus in Prague
1415 Henry V wins at Agincourt and crushes the Lollards	1415 The burning of John Hus
Henry of Beaufort in Bohemia	1420 *The Hussite Revolution*
The War of the Barons	
	1458 King George: Pacification of the country
1485 Henry VII Tudor monarchy established	1466 First Czech printed book Religious tolerance law Weak kings of the Jagellon dynasty
1529 Henry VIII English reformation	1526 Louis of Jagellon killed in a struggle with the Turks Hapsburg dynasty: Ferdinand I
1588 Elizabeth Spanish Armada	Maximilian II Rudolph II at Prague
1603 James Stuart King of Scotland and England 1613 Princess Elizabeth marries Frederick of the Palatinate	1609 The Letter of Majesty
1618 Death of Walter Raleigh	1618 The Defenestration of Prague 1619 Frederick elected King of Bohemia in stead of Ferdinand II
1620 Volunteers sent to Bohemia Pilgrim Fathers leave for America Charles I Charles' personal rule	1620 Battle of White Mountain The end of the old Bohemia 1626 Mansfeld's campaign through Moravia 1634 Death of Wallenstein *Thirty Years' War*
1640 *The English Revolution*	1641 Comenius visits England 1648 The Treaty of Westphalia
1649 Execution of Charles I Oliver Cromwell's Protectorate 1660 Restoration of Charles II 1688 Revolution: William III King Wars against France	Religious persecution Decline of intellectual life Turkish wars Wars against France

1714	The Hanoverians: George I		Charles VI, the last Hapsburg
		1740	Maria Theresa
1745	Highland Rebellion Wars against France	1745	Final loss of Silesia Seven Years' War The further decline of Bohemia
1776	Declaration of American Independence	1781	Patent of Toleration Czech national revival begins
1789	French Revolution Wars against France		Joseph II Wars against France
1805	Battle of Trafalgar	1805	Battle of Slavkov (Austerlitz)
	English Industrial Revolution		
1832	First Reform Bill	1832	Bowring's Cheskian Anthology published
		1844	Slovak literary language established
1846	Repeal of Corn Laws	1848	Slavonic Congress in Prague First Austrian Parliament
	Queen Victoria American Civil War	1850	T. G. Masaryk born in Hodonín Beginnings of parliamentarism
	Formation of German Empire	1867	The Ausgleich – Czech rights denied by the Hapsburgs
	Spanish-American and Boer Wars	1882	Prague University divided Industrialisation of Bohemia and Moravia
		1907	Reform of electoral law
1914	First World War starts	1915	Masaryk starts the national struggle for independence
1917	U. S. declares war on Germany	1917	Allies declare the liberation of the Czechs and Slovaks one of peace terms
1918	Armistice Treaty of Versailles	1918	Establishment of free and independent Czechoslovakia Building of the state
	Decline of democratic Europe begins		Sudeten Germans turn Nazi
1933	Hitler seizes power in Germany		
1935	Italo-Abyssinian War War in Spain	1935	Mutual assistance pact between Czechoslovakia and U. S. S. R.
1938	The Munich Crisis	1938	Sudetenland ceded
1939	Britain declares war on Germany	1939	Czechoslovakia seized Beginnings of the terror
1940	Czechs fight in the Battle of Britain	1940	President Beneš in London Exiled government established Czechoslovak government recognized by the United Nations
1941	Soviet Russia and the United States enter the war		
1942	Atlantic Charter	1942	Reign of terror: Lidice destroyed
1943	Conference in Moscow	1943	Soviet-Czechoslovak Treaty of Alliance
1944	Invasion	1944	Slovak Rising
1945	Second World War brought to an end	1945	Liberation of Czechoslovakia

BOHEMIA
INTERNATIONAL

JOSEF VINCENT POLIŠENSKÝ

HISTORY OF CZECHOSLOVAKIA IN OUTLINE

Vydala Bohemia International,
nakladatelství,
s. p., Zahraniční literatura.
Grafická úprava Josef Týfa.
Praha 1991.
Tisk Svoboda, grafické závody, a. s.
Praha 10.
Vydání druhé (v Bohemii první).